My Father's Compass

The fifth in a family of four children, Howard Goldenberg was born in Melbourne but made – with all Australian parts – in Leeton, New South Wales.

On his father's side, he is descended from the Gaon (Genius) of Vilna, and on his mother's from Cyril Coleman, pearl diver, polo player and one-stringed violinist, of Broome.

In 1974, together with Joseph John Mann, Howard founded the Stomach Club of Australasia, a body which he guided over the next quarter century from strength to weakness to extinction.

In a low-budget cottage industry, labouring in the marital trenches, employing the most modest of equipment, quite without fanfare or government subsidy, Howard participated with his wife Annette in the production of Rachel, Raphael and Naomi. Forbearing to dispose of this litter, the couple have since been rewarded by the advent of five adorable grandchildren.

Howard has run thirty-six full marathons and sixty-one laps around the sun.

He is engaged in fulfilling his life's ambition to become a promising young writer.

His mother is proud of him.

Howard Goldenberg

MY FATHER'S
C⊛MPASS
A Memoir

Published by Hybrid Publishers

Melbourne Victoria Australia

© Howard Goldenberg

First published 2007

National Library of Australia Cataloguing-in-Publication data:

Goldenberg, Howard.

My father's compass : a memoir.

ISBN 9781876462482.

1. Goldenberg, Myer, 1910- . 2. Goldenberg, Howard. 3. Fathers and
sons - Biography. I. Title.

920.71

Editor: Anna Rosner Blay
Cover design: Ann Likhovetsky
Photographs: Courtesy of the author
Typeset in 12/16.5 pt Adobe Garamond Pro
Printed in Australia by Ligare

Contents

To Annette

Acknowledgments

I acknowledge that these memories are mine and that others will recall events differently. When Dad read these stories of his life he used to say I had a wonderful imagination. I hope my sister and brothers will be as indulgent as our father was. I know that Mum will.

For more than three years, this slim book has taken my time and my attention from people I love – as well as from chores I do not love. I acknowledge the forbearance of my loved ones and their support of an enterprise that was fulfilling to me alone.

Numerous very private people have tolerated the acts of writing and publishing their personal material with uncommon grace. They have only my love as recompense – and my heartfelt thanks.

I acknowledge with gratitude the generosity of Helen Garner and Martin Flanagan whose occasional pithy advice resulted in the removal of a good deal of schmaltz from my writing.

It was the novelist Brendan Gullifer who remarked that writing was much like digesting – everyone can do it, but it's difficult to sell the product. Brendan never ceased encouraging me to find a buyer for the product.

In the event, I found a publisher in Louis de Vries and an editor in Anna Rosner Blay, the former a thorough gentleman, the latter an editor of great skill and tact. Only a person struggling as I have to become a promising young writer could appreciate the contribution of these two to this book.

Last mentioned, most loved – my wife, Annette; in the act of writing a memoir the writer turns his attention backwards in time. In this process the present is disregarded and the future is nowhere in view. A writer's spouse, meanwhile, has ample opportunity to regard the writer's posterior, patiently awaiting a resumption of the present and dreaming of the future.

I have looked back well and truly. I have recalled and recounted these tales. I have honoured their subject and now have freed myself of the burden of the tale.

I turn around at last and it is Annette whom I see – and whom I embrace.

Howard Goldenberg
Melbourne, February 2007

Preface

When I was a young boy, two great storytellers told me great stories.

Dad was the teller of the stories of the Bible – the stories of Abraham and his two sons, of Isaac and his two sons, and of Jacob and his twelve sons. All those sons quarrelled and fought – just like my brothers and me.

And the stories of David, who was small, and Goliath who was big and mean. David, being brave, fought against Goliath and beat him. That gave me hope that one day I might be brave and strong enough to beat my big brother in a fight.

My Dad could tell these stories by heart. After he had listened to us say the *Shema Yisrael* prayer in bed at night, with the light out, he would tell us those old stories.

The stories were new every time, and Dad's voice was the deep voice of God speaking to Jacob at Beth El, and to Moses from the burning bush. When God called the young boy Samuel in the middle of the night, it was Dad who replied, 'Here I am'. Dad was in the voice of that lonely child in the deep crypts of the great house of God.

And when Elijah was alone in the wilderness, chased and hunted because he spoke out against wickedness, he heard the still, soft voice of God and we heard Dad's voice in our dark bedroom. And when Nathan thundered his accusation at the mighty king, Dad's was the voice in the thunder.

On *Shabbat*, Dad would read the Bible stories to us from the great big fat book of *Tanach* he was given for his bar mitzvah. You could feel the passion in those stories that Dad read to us; Dad's voice throbbed with life and death. It ached with love, whined with envy or rang with faith and courage.

This was my introduction to the power and drama of stories.

Meanwhile, Mummy was telling stories of another sort. Hers were the stories of imagination and make believe. Magic lived in every rise and fall of that champagne voice. We walked the yellow brick road, we faced pirates on Treasure Island, we were beset by legion wicked witches who ate, poisoned, stole or bewitched little children.

Although we encountered wickedness of every variety, we learned that goodness and bravery and cleverness might yet win the day – and that magic was everywhere, always possible.

I knew that ultimately evil must be feeble, because the voice that told the stories was the voice of my own mother, the voice that said, 'You are safe in this world.'

By night the voice of my father and by day the voice of my mother fed my mind and made my world bigger, took me into times long past and into places that never were but still might be. I was a little boy in a small town, but I travelled a wide world and the reaches of eternity. Life had no limits for a boy in the arms of a parent, in the thrall of the tale, in the music of the telling.

Although the stories boldly told of the evil in the universe and the darkness at the heart of man, the very act of storytelling told me too that all things were possible, even the triumph of goodness. The giant and the ogre and the witch and the taskmaster were horrible, but they didn't rule the world.

You might be good. You could be great. You were safe.

Stories are stored in books and inside the memories of grown-ups. When a grown-up cuddles you on a knee, when the storyteller's breast is against your back and big arms encircle you with a book held in front of you, you are inside an embrace, inside a world. In the circle of those arms you are travelling together on a magic carpet through the story. You never forget the enchantment, you never stop feeling that embrace. The story and the storyteller and you are bound together.

Later, new magic happens: you start to read. Soon you realise you can read a story without the help of a grown-up. And when you have read a few stories and retold some of them, you discover that you can even make up stories of your own.

Stories can do magical things. They can remind a grown-up person that there is a little child inside who waits and hungers for enchantment, longing to be set free. Once you find that you have a story to tell, you need someone to sit and listen, and to share the tale. That's why we have children when we grow up – because grown-ups love stories.

All my little children have grown up, and I now have grandchildren to tell the stories to.

Come. I'll tell you a story. It's about my father.

Prologue: Learning To Be a Son

Myer Goldenberg was born on 5 December 1910. In January 1946, when his second son was born, Myer was thirty-five years old. Over the following fifty-seven and a half years the father and that son would engage in an intense relationship, both striving always to improve, both aware of a sense of anxious imperfection.

That each loved the other deeply, neither ever doubted. On the water, in the confines of a motor car, in storytelling and at prayer, they played out their respective apprenticeships as father and as son.

The boy became a man, the father aged; the son became a father; the father's powers began, at the last, to fail. Then the father died.

I am that son.

This is the story of those fifty-seven and a half years.

One

A Good Jewish Boy

My father was a faithful Jew. He was also a radical sceptic: he never believed anything he was told without seeing the evidence for himself, and sifting and weighing it. Notwithstanding his scepticism, he observed the commandments through his long life.

Dad held certain precepts higher than others: Honour your father and your mother *was probably the script of my father's life. He wished to be worthy of his parents, whom he venerated.*

In turn, Dad demanded that we children honour him and Mum – especially him. Where the fifth commandment said honour your father *before mentioning* your mother, *Dad drew an inference of male precedence. Dad honoured his own father as a patriarch and came to be a patriarch in his own right. Honouring our parents meant obeying them, not raising a hand to them, not even raising our voices to them in anger. My father practised that commandment to a degree that was almost unbearable.*

Late in the final year of his life, my father made his way to the lectern at the front of the synagogue to lead the prayers. The occasion was the anniversary of the death of his mother. Every year on that date, Dad led the prayers in a public act of filial honour. Now my father was frail, breathless on the least exertion, subject to devastating loss of balance and humiliating falls. Through all this, he clung to the lectern and gave voice. The congregation, most of them his junior by one, two or even three generations, witnessed the struggle. No eye could be torn from my father. The service was breathless, all were moved and many appalled by this venerable man in his act of inescapable loyalty.

This was the forty-second anniversary of Nanny's death. A week later, my father fell at home – attempting chivalrously to care for my mother's carer – and sustained injuries that saw him hospitalised. He never recovered.

I think that Dad valued duty to a parent above even dedication to a spouse. Certainly, when I married Annette my father acted as one betrayed; and when my sister – always so dutiful and loving towards him – made her life in America at the side of her husband, Dad seemed baffled by her 'perfidy'.

Being a good boy or a naughty boy was a moral state with a religious dimension. To use swear words, for example, would be to move away from goodness; to help an old lady across the road was to enter a state of grace.

Unlike other strict religious codes, the Goldenberg code had little to say about Heaven, and less about Hell. Theological guilt and anxiety were not dominant motivators; being close to Dad was my heaven – being held at a distance was perdition. There was always the knowledge that redemption was at hand; I only had to try harder, then Dad would see and understand, and I would return to favour in his eyes.

I embraced this strict code naturally and happily. I learned that my father wished me to go beyond the mere formal respect prescribed in our religious rituals (which are both hierarchical and male supremacist), to acts of gift and of tribute to our inherited identity. In this respect I was a loyal Jew before I was a believer. Similarly, I suspect that my father's adherence to tradition and observance was at least as much an adherence to his father as to the Deity.

As a small child I found it unrewarding to contest too strenuously any issue with my father. If I happened to cross the line into

4

disrespect, I would experience a distance from Dad that was painfully lonely. By contrast, being a timorous and needy young boy, I found that honouring my father was deeply satisfying. 'Good boy, Howard' was a balm; and as often as not it was elaborated to: 'Good Jewish boy, Howard'. When I heard these words, I knew I had joined Dad intimately in the line of love, observance and loyalty that linked him to his father – and with all the fathers right back to Abraham – and that I had a secure place and footing in this world.

Hay and Hell

One summer's day, Dad takes us to the big canal near Jack Harris' farm. This flows all the way to Hay, ninety miles away. Dad warns us that if a child were to fall into the water, the strong current would catch him and carry him downstream towards Hay. Jack Harris and Dad sometimes take us sailing on the Hay Canal in Wamoon, four miles from Leeton. But today the yacht is not on the canal.

Dad explains, 'We are not sailing today; we are going to aqua-plane.'

Jack Harris' truck is up on the bank of the canal. There is a long cable that runs from the back of the truck to a board floating near the bank. I stand near the water's edge and watch Dad mount the board and grab hold of the two short ropes that are secured to the top of the board in front of him. Suddenly the engine of Jack's truck roars above me, and at the same moment the cable tightens and Dad is gone in a surge of wash below. Jack's truck is racing along the bank, and Dad and the board are flashes of silver over the waters that are lit by the sun upon the face of the canal.

Then Dad is lost.

After a few minutes the truck returns. On its tray are the board and the cable and Dad. On Dad's face is the smile of one who has tasted bliss. 'That is aquaplaning,' he says. Then Dad lugs that board back into the water, and instead of re-mounting it, he lifts me from the bank onto the plank. The plank tilts, water comes over the top and I slide forward into the water, the swift-flowing waters which will snatch me away to Hay and – who knows? – beyond Hay to Booligal, and to Hell as well.

Dad plucks me from the water and from eternity and climbs back onto the plank, placing me securely between his legs. He places my hands around the ropes and grasps them firmly in his own hands as well. I am shivering.

Jack's truck roars, the board leaps beneath us and we are airborne. We are flight, we are speed and light, we are lost to sight, beyond the world. We are aquaplaning at top speed downstream towards Hay. In defiance of all danger and drowning, I am safe in the grasp of my father.

❇

When the Nestlé people devise sweetened condensed milk they are actually creating cans packed with the primal pleasure of my life – I mean milk – and supercharging it with sugar. The result is a smooth, thick fluid of such overpowering sweetness that it exists squarely on the border of delight and amazement. Mum has just opened a can of this nectar and, like sin, it coucheth near the door in the kitchen of our home at Number 10 Wade Avenue, Leeton, New South Wales.

We have just finished eating our lunch, a meat meal. I have learned from Dad the Jewish dietary law that forbids us to eat dairy food for the next three hours after meat. I know the law, but on this occasion it simply slips my mind and I decide that a spoonful of Nestlés is my dessert. The spoon is already in my mouth when Dad's eye meets mine from across the room.

'You are a *goy*,' he says, and turns away.

Stunned, I do not understand immediately what I have done, only that somehow I must have renounced the faith of my forefathers. What I do know is that my own father has withdrawn his love.

I am adrift. Without Dad's love, I will float fast away – beyond Hay, beyond all knowing – to Hell.

Burned!

Fire fascinates us. Adults make our fires – in the fireplace in our lounge room and under the billy at picnics and great big roaring bonfires for Empire Day – but we children aren't allowed to make fires. Or even to touch matches; we have to pass the box to Dad unopened. Rarely Dad will say to one of us, 'Open the box and hand me one match.' Then with that solitary match Dad conjures a grand blaze in the lounge.

Children mustn't touch fire: fire can kill and destroy.

But fire fascinates us terribly. That fascination explains our smoking; when we roll bits of torn newspaper into cigarettes, then light them and inhale, we certainly don't do it for pleasure – the taste is rank and the aroma is fierce.

We create fire because we can, because we must. When Dad forbids us to play with fire, his voice is heavy with danger and his gaze is terrible with grown-up knowledge. I haven't seen a house burn down but I do know how a father's anger can burn.

For this reason we light our fires only on Wednesdays. Wednesdays are good for fires because that's when Dad goes fishing. He goes with Tom Saunderson to a secret place – a billabong on the Murrumbidgee – where the farmer lets them onto his land and they fish illegally with gill nets.

It is Wednesday and school has finished. Dennis, my friend Johnny Wanklyn and I build a bonfire in our backyard. We boil a billy and make tea, a novel drink whose taste you have to drown with sugar. All of this is pretty brave and adventurous stuff. We are hardy men of the Outback, manly and independent. After a while the tea acts powerfully upon our bladders and we relieve ourselves onto the flames, amazed by the pungent fumes that rise from the blackened logs.

Mum calls us inside for dinner and we extinguish the embers with water from the garden hose, then cover the ashes with soil from the garden. We sit at the dinner table, smeared with soot and smelling of smoke. As usual, Mum asks no questions. But after the meal she says, 'Wash your hair in the bath tonight, boys.'

By the time the fisherman returns from his poaching it is dark, and Dad finds his two elder sons lying in bed, apparently asleep, washed clean of smoke and soot. The poacher, preoccupied with his catch of cod and perch, scales and cleans his fish and buries the guts. He does not notice the garden bed smoking mysteriously in the dark.

The next morning I awaken early and creep outside in the half light to inspect the patch of warm soil from which wisps of smoke still rise. My leg bumps into the cast-iron tripod that supported our billy above the flames yesterday. The metal is still warm, hot in fact. It leaves a hot patch on the skin of my left calf which I barely notice as I run inside to say my morning prayers.

As I dress for school, that hot patch is harder to ignore. It gives a very strong sensation and, what is worse, it betrays me with a dark mark on the skin, the imprint of a hot iron bar. This could be serious. I run to the bathroom and lock the door. Here, I make frantic efforts to wash away the evidence. But the deep red mark remains.

I pull my school sock high on my calf to cover the burn, then sit and writhe, waiting for Dad to take us to school in his car. I am looking forward keenly to school today: even a pain-filled day of reading, writhing and arithmetic is preferable to discovery by Dad of our Wednesday fire-making.

Dad drives us to school. We climb out of the car but, before I can bolt, Dad calls me back. I know I am discovered. I try to walk without limping. 'What do you want, Dad?' I ask, knowing that what he wants is my hide.

'You forgot my kiss goodbye,' says Dad. Gratefully I oblige, then turn to go. At this stage, my sock works itself free of its constraining garter and falls down, revealing my well-turned ankle and my well-burned calf.

A voice calls from the car and I return, defeated. 'Show me your leg … that's a burn,' says my father, my doctor. 'Get into the car.' I do so, trying not to look up at his face. The car travels only a very short distance. When it stops I follow that voice into a large building which I recognise as the Leeton and District Hospital. Only a month ago we came here to visit Mum and the new baby. Is Mum in here again, having another baby? No, it is not Mum who is the patient today but I.

We have arrived in another part of the hospital where I smell anaesthetic ether. There are nurses here wearing masks, and instruments and bandages. A nurse brings a tube of cream. I am shaking as Dad takes some of the cream and applies it to my burn. Then Dad asks for a bandage which he wraps around my creamed burned leg. Dad's deft hands are firm and gentle. The dressing is cool and my leg feels better. I sneak a look upwards and see no cloud of anger, only concern and love.

Dad takes me to the car, drives me the short distance to school and kisses me goodbye for a second time. He asks no questions.

Shouting

Dennis and I sit in the dark kitchen in East St Kilda where Nanny is giving us our breakfast. From somewhere out of sight around dark corners in the large house, I can hear Papa shouting. The sounds come closer and now Papa stands at the door, shouting at Nanny as the little room fills with roaring angry sounds.

Now Nanny is shouting too: 'No, Joe! No!' Her voice is high and trembly. They are both shouting at once, Nanny standing just at my side, Papa in the doorway, and the world is too small.

I look up at Nanny. There are tears in her eyes. I look across the table, away from Nanny to the Early Kooka oven door. There is a worm in the mouth of the kookaburra. Papa has stopped shouting. Nanny is crying in small gulping sobs.

On the gas stove, the kettle is singing. From a milk bottle, Nanny pours half a cup of milk each for Dennis and me, then tops up the milk with water from the kettle. Nanny and Papa do this because full strength milk is wasteful and because it is too rich for small children. At home in Leeton we drink it straight.

Dennis and I drink our thin Melbourne milk and Nanny reaches into her apron for her hanky. She blows her nose. Dennis gets up and goes over to Nanny. He puts his arms around her.

Afterwards we go upstairs. In the big empty rooms I can feel a large ball in my throat. I start to cry. Dennis goes to get Nanny and she says I am homesick and I am missing my mother and father. She gives me some paper and a pencil so I can write them a letter.

The lump in my throat gets bigger. I have never written a letter. I start to write but then I just cry instead. My tears fall onto the paper and make a smudge on 'Dear Mummy and Daddy'. I tear up the paper and Papa comes upstairs to take my letter to the post office, and when he sees that I have wasted the paper he shouts at me.

Uncle Abe comes to the big house in East St Kilda to visit his parents. He speaks to Papa, Papa shouts at him, then Uncle Abe shouts at Nanny. He is shouting and Nanny is shouting but they are both smiling. Afterwards Uncle Abe explains: 'Nanny is deaf; she can't hear me if I don't shout.'

Uncle Abe takes me in his car. We spend a whole day together and I help Uncle Abe with his work; he lets me steer the car and work the horn. We eat sandwiches together and I am his helper. Later he tells me stories from the olden days about my Papa, Joseph Goldenberg.

'Do you know how Papa came to Australia? He ran away from his home and stowed away on a ship. His mother had died and his father's new wife was unkind to him, so he decided to leave Israel – he was only twelve years old when he ran away from home.'

I sit and think about Papa. It is hard to imagine my fierce grand-father as a little boy. Would he have felt lonely, a boy living far from his home without a mother and a father, without his brothers and sisters? Did someone give him milk to drink?

'Then, when he was nineteen, he met Nanny in Ballarat. Nanny had a great big family and when he was with them it was the first time he had a family life in this country. He married Nanny, and soon he and Nanny had three little boys and Papa wasn't lonely any more.'

I need to know why Papa shouts so much. Uncle Abe looks thoughtful. He clasps the back of my neck with his big hand and squeezes me firmly. His hand is strong from his work on the family farm. It feels warm and gentle on my neck.

'When Papa shouts he still loves us. He loves us all dearly.' It still doesn't make sense to me. Uncle Abe looks at something a long way away. '*Boychick*,' he says, 'Papa is full of strong warm feelings. It doesn't take much to make the feelings hot and then they boil over. He's like a kettle that's too full and too hot.'

'Does he shout at Daddy?'

'Sometimes. But he is very proud of your father. He feels proud of your dad's education, and what a good doctor he is. You know Papa had to leave school when he was only nine. So all his children and all his grandchildren have chances that he never had. He wanted us to succeed so much that he boiled over quite often.'

Back home in Leeton no one shouts much – except for Old Bowp-Bowp next door. Old Bowp-Bowp is as old as Papa, but much more fearsome. When he shouts at me, I know it is not because he is boil-ing over with love.

Old Bowp-Bowp sells Volkswagen and Mercedes cars and owns the hearse that takes dead people to the cemetery. Outside his house he has a large ornamental pool. On a warm day that pool in his front yard looks cool and inviting.

One hot day Dennis and I visit his pool and jump in for a cooling dip. The old man comes running out of the house, roaring at the top of his voice. As he runs he unbuckles the belt that holds his trousers to his giant belly. He pulls the belt free and makes lashing movements with it as he runs towards us.

I sit in his pool, paralysed with fear, mesmerised by the strange sounds he's making; it sounds like 'Bowp! Bowp!' to me. Dennis grabs my hand and pulls it, saving me from the foaming undertaker.

Later, safely in hiding in the shrubbery at the back of our garden, I try to make out the old man's words: they might have been 'Get Out! Get Out!' From that time Dennis and I call him Old Bowp-Bowp. When we are feeling brave we run past his front gate, yelling out that name.

When our oldest cousin, Barry the Big, visits us, we tell him about Old Bowp-Bowp. Barry's curiosity is aroused. He visits the old man's pool to hear the words for himself. When the old man screams at Barry, Barry just shouts 'Bowp! Bowp!' back at him at the top of his voice. The undertaker charges towards the pool, but Barry just sits there shouting at him.

Watching in terror from the gate, I pray for Barry in what must be his final living moments with an undertaker. At the last moment, Barry leaps from the pool and runs. But the old man has anticipated this and has cut off Barry's escape. Then Barry turns and runs around the pool's perimeter *towards* the house. The old man turns and chases him but Barry is too quick and now skips blithely through the unguarded gate, calling out 'Bowp! Bowp!' as he goes. It is thrilling to watch.

There's not much shouting in our home. Mummy has a soft voice. I don't think she knows how to shout. Dad knows how to shout. Sometimes he shouts at Dennis – when Dennis does something he doesn't like. He didn't like it when Dennis took me into Dad's surgery and showed me how to pump up the blood pressure machine. There are numbers on the machine. Dennis said, 'I bet I can pump it up to 300,' and he did. Dennis kept pumping until the rubber burst and mercury went flying all around the room.

Later Dad found the broken blood pressure machine. He shouted then. But he doesn't often need to shout at me. He only has to look at me and say quietly and slowly and clearly, *'How dare you!'* and I don't dare at all.

On Thursday nights, Dennis and I go to Cubs. It's Boy Scouts for kids younger than ten. One Thursday night we come home early from Cubs and as we approach the front door I can hear shouting from inside. When we let ourselves in, the shouting stops. Mummy has been crying and Dad's voice is husky. They look after us, gratefully, helping us into our pyjamas as if we were still little babies.

As Daddy tucks me in, he says something to explain the shouting. I don't understand it. I understand only that my parents were very angry at each other and it frightens me. Then Mummy comes and kisses me goodnight. She starts to explain but I don't want to hear it. For some reason I feel afraid to understand.

I do understand one thing: I don't like shouting. If I am a good boy Daddy won't boil over and he won't shout at me. So I try very, very hard to become a good boy.

Bathing with my brother

Big Barry is down from Melbourne. Barry is our hero. He spends his daytimes here touring Leeton by car. Barry is eleven years old and wealthy. So wealthy is he that he can pay Dennis and me to push him in our pedal car up and down the streets of our town, doling out lollies which he buys at the milk bar in Pine Avenue for twopence a pack of twelve. Barry buys twelve packs a day at a daily cost of two shillings. This requires him to go through 144 lollies between breakfast and teatime – a formidable task with which we assist him as we take turns to push.

When the light fades and the lollies run out, we come back home.

After a day of touring we have little appetite. We are all tired and dusty so Mum sends us to take a bath.

It was in this bathroom only a few nights ago that Barry explained to us how babies are made. Such extraordinary knowledge deepens our admiration for our cousin and now, more than ever, we look to him for ideas and leadership.

We are seated in the bath, three small boys, alone and naked. I notice that Barry is doing something unusual: he is soaping himself. More particularly, he is soaping his genitals. He looks up and asks, 'Den, Doff – do you want to learn a new game? It's called Murder in the Chook House.' We do want to learn the game.

Barry says, 'I'll show you how to play it,' then, covering his genitals with one hand, he lunges forward and grabs suddenly for Dennis' penis. As he clutches it, he gives it a mighty tweak and cries out, 'Murder in the Chook House!'

Dennis is surprised; I am amazed. And awestruck by the beauty and simplicity of the game. I am also unprepared for the next phase. While I sit in a state of high hilarity and watch Dennis crouching low, gingerly and tenderly counting his blessings, Big Barry leans in my direction, reaches downwards, secures a firm grip and yanks sharply upwards. Once again the cry rings out: 'Murder in the Chook House!'

Now it is my turn to be surprised. And to reflect that the simple game is not always so beautiful. While I am nursing my injured privates back to health, Dennis regains his sense of humour and convulses with unattractive mirth, holding his hands ever firmly in his lap.

There is a pause. Three small naked boys sit still and recover their breath and consider. Then, united, two smaller figures leap upon the larger and attempt to disembowel him. But Big Barry's covering grip is strong and it takes a period of concerted effort for the four smaller hands to dislodge the larger two. Finally, two voices pipe out their cry of victory, but 'Murder …' dies in their throats as their hands slip in futility from the well-soaped genitalia of their cunning cousin.

This game is much less simple than I first thought. And more dangerous, as the bathroom door opens and an adult enters. It is Mum. She looks at us, sees us seated demurely with our hands in our laps, ponders a bit and smiles. Then she says mildly, 'Be careful not to damage yourselves, boys.' Mum turns to go, stops and says, 'You had better keep the noise down. It's six o'clock.' The door closes behind her.

'What happens at six o'clock?' asks Barry.

'It's Dad's surgery hours,' we explain, 'and we aren't allowed to make a noise because he is seeing sick people. He's two rooms away and if we disturb him he'll kill us.'

Another pause, then Barry gets up from the bath, goes to the door and turns a key in the lock. We have never noticed that lock before. He gets back into the bath and, before he can cover his bases, Dennis and I attack, grasp, shriek in triumph; then gasp as Barry counterattacks successfully. In the minutes that follow there is murder on all sides in the Chook House in the bathroom. Water flies in all directions, heavy casualties are sustained as privates are taken prisoner and released; the evening rings with the sounds of mayhem, of grief and relief. Bodies leap, slip, twist and writhe, and chests heave and throats burn in an ecstasy of bloodlust, treachery and revenge.

A sound penetrates. Over the din it is heard again. It is a knocking, loud and imperative, at the bathroom door. Dad's voice is heard, the voice of cold command, not loud but austere. It says: 'Unlock The Door.'

We look at Barry. Barry is on his feet. Dad enters as Barry resumes his position at one end of the bath, and Dad looks about him. There is water everywhere, but almost none of it in the bath. There are three small boys, naked, seated in a tub, their hands all in their laps. The boys are breathing heavily.

There is no smile on Dad's face. For a moment he does not speak. He looks long at me, looks at Dennis, then at Barry. He says, 'There is a sick person in my surgery. I need quiet.' A sick person, no doubt very sick, no doubt in danger because of our noise.

'There had better be quiet,' says Dad with an intensity that frightens me more than a raised voice or a raised hand. Then, 'Who locked that door? I don't want that door locked again … finish your bath now, then get out and dry yourselves. You're getting cold. I don't want you to get sick.'

Dad goes to his very sick person. We are very quiet so he can save a life. A full minute passes, then it is time for us to take life and to save our own. Quietly, desperately, without need of announcement – under threat of pain unnamed from Dad – murder resumes in the Chook House. Dennis (assuming my constancy and support) throws himself upon Big Barry. At this moment, while his defences are down, I find it opportune to attack Dennis from the flank. Then Barry and Dennis join in coalition against me, but they find the target small and elusive; the cold has worked in my favour. Meanwhile, my own smaller hands find their way and work their magic, and big brother and bigger cousin defend frantically.

Allegiances form and fall away. All is fluid as three small bodies strain and thrash and scream 'Murder!' in whispers, in exultation and in terror on the very extreme of this life's existence.

I feel rather than hear the fall of heavy footsteps. The others sense it too. We are on our feet, out of the bath, towelling ourselves in urgent silence.

For the remainder of the week, Mum supervises our bath hour more closely. At the end of the week, Barry's tour of Leeton is over, his funds exhausted, and he goes back to Melbourne and to his higher education in human biology.

Never again do we play Murder in the Chook House! And never do we forget that purple evening – at least Big Barry and Dennis and I never forget. I don't know whether Dad remembers; although it was he who electrified our game, I never discuss it with him.

Bathing with my brother – II

Our parents like us to take a bath every day. They are thinking of cleanliness and godliness. Dennis and I like the bath for quite different reasons; when you are six and four, there are lots of games you can play in a bath. The greatest of these is Murder in the Chook House, a spirited bath game for three or more players that Big Barry taught us.

But Barry has gone back to Melbourne, leaving Dennis and me to our own resources. We sit down in the warm water, and – quicker than thought – I empty my bladder. I watch the yellow stain swell and fade before me as it disperses in the tub, flowing palely towards my brother. Dennis has not noticed that he is bathing in my wee. I enjoy the knowledge quietly.

Then Dennis proposes a new game. 'Howard,' he says, 'let's do something new. Let's take it in turns to put our penises in each other's mouths …'

This *is* new. It's a long way from cleanliness and further still from godliness. It is breathtakingly naughty. It is irresistible.

Dennis outlines his idea: 'Howard, I'll put mine in your mouth first, then we'll swap.'

'What if Dad catches us?'

The words are no sooner out of my mouth than Dennis is out of the bath and – in breach of a recent rule – locks the bathroom door from the inside. We are alone and safe from discovery. Then another danger surfaces in my trembling mind: 'How do I know you won't wee in my mouth?'

The question gives Dennis pause. Then he says, 'I wouldn't do that; if I did, you would only wee in my mouth later, when it's your turn.'

A good answer, but I know my brother. I sit and think, then I recall that (unusually) Dennis has not peed in the bath tonight. He is holding it in. He is Planning Something.

'No,' I say, 'I don't trust you. You're keeping your wee to trick me.'

Pale at my unfair accusation, Dennis now rises on his haunches and pees virtuously into the water between us. Then he takes the soap, washes his doodle thoroughly and rinses it off. He looks up and delivers a stirring speech: 'See, Howard? I'm empty and clean. You're safe. Let's do it. What do you say?'

Moments later, Dennis is at my end of the bath, on his haunches again, jockeying delicately into the correct anatomic position. He leans his head and trunk back slightly to allow himself to fall into place, when I pull my own head back abruptly and turn aside.

'What's wrong now?' he asks.

'I bet you've saved some wee. I reckon you're going to pee inside me.'

'Never!'

'Well don't try it — or I'll bite!'

Pale again, Dennis pauses, then nods, and works his way forward and repeats the docking procedure. This time I open my mouth and then, between my tongue and palate I feel something: a bit like a marshmallow only firmer, and slippery. It is a novel sensation. Now my mouth fills with something warm and bitter. I am confused, then the thought, the certainty hits me: Dennis, my older brother, my flesh and blood, is using my mouth as a toilet!

'YOU PEED! YOU BROKE YOUR PROMISE!'

I spit, then slam my upper and lower teeth savagely together. But Dennis has gone. In a deft and delicate manoeuvre he has backed, swivelled and made his light escape into the beautiful. He sits at his end of the bath, a hyena, laughing hideously.

Dennis recovers from his helpless mirth. 'My turn!' I cry.

'No,' says Dennis, 'I'm getting out now.'

Oh Dad, where are you when I need you?

Trust

My father taught all of his children how to navigate using a compass. He showed us how the compass needle, under the influence of the earth's magnetic pole, always pointed north; and how we could use that constancy to work out all other directions.

Then he added one striking fact: this generally dependable north-seeking needle obeyed a magnetic force, but under certain extreme conditions this north, this magnetic north, was not true north.

In a lifetime with my father, I saw that his own north was proof against corrupting influence. As much as Dad was a man of faith, he was a man of good faith. In a long and honoured medical career, in business, in marriage and in all his relationships, trust was a virtue that Dad held sacred.

When he died, his family engraved a tribute upon his tombstone, a tribute to this remarkable integrity:

> ... *he walked honestly,*
> *he worked righteously,*
> *and spoke his heart's truth.*

The officiating rabbi, an old friend and patient, read the citation and remarked: 'That was Myer Goldenberg – straight as an arrow.'

To my enduring mild surprise, our father truly believed in my own literal truthfulness. Equally phenomenal – given my general deviousness – is the fact that I never did in fact lie to our father.

Curiously, Dad felt that Her Majesty's Royal Mail was sacred; he assured us that he would not under any circumstance open or read another person's mail.

'Not even our mail?' I wondered.

'No, Howard, not yours, not anyone's.'

An amazing thought: grown-ups have rules that even they must obey.

My word

'Jump in and swim to me, Howard.'

Dad treads water near the bank of the irrigation canal. Somehow he remains afloat, somehow he stays put in the racing current. He calls out again, encouraging me: 'Come on, Howard – you can do it.'

The water looks deep. Back in the pool at Yanco I can dog paddle all the way across from one side to the other; but this canal is a stranger, its waters dark, alive. The grey-green depths are sullen and threatening. I remember John Morrison, Dad's friend, smiling John, John with the brilliantined hair …

Dad's voice is confident. He says, 'Jump in and swim, Howard, just like you do at Yanco pool.'

'I can't, Dad …'

'Yes you can, darling.'

'I'm scared …'

'You don't need to be afraid. I'll look after you. Jump in and swim to me and I'll hold you and look after you.'

'Do you promise, Dad?'

Dad's eyes widen. His voice changes. He leans forward in my direction and he gazes at me, into me. He is fifteen yards away but he is holding me already. His voice is a whisper, a caress, a *command*: 'I've given you my word, Howard. *My word is sufficient.* You don't need me to promise.'

I jump in. The water is around me and on top of me. The whole world is grey-green and I cannot see the bank, I cannot see Dad. When I break the surface, Dad is over there, near the bank, his arms outstretched, and I am paddling, paddling frantically, and Dad is closer. A few more strokes and I will be safe.

Dad calls, 'Keep going, Howard, keep swimming, you're doing well.' Dad's arms reach for me, but every yard I swim forward, Dad seems to recede a little. Confounded, frightened, I stop swimming

20

and cry out. Then the gap disappears and Dad holds me. His Sunday face is unshaven and I feel his bristles against my cheek and his voice is in my ear: 'I gave you my word; you don't need to be afraid. And you are a good swimmer.'

✳

Dennis hurries across the hallway towards me. He beckons me close and whispers. He has an idea for a new game: 'Howard,' he says, 'why don't you go up to Dad and say "Up your bum!"'

I look at Dad, standing at the far end of the hall. Dad does not like rude words. He doesn't want me to play with Tony Iano because Tony teaches me words like *bum* and *bloody* and *dick*. I can imagine how Dad will react if I say those words to him.

'No,' I say to Dennis, 'I'm not going to say that. Why don't you say it?'

Dennis gives the matter some thought, then says, 'Perhaps you're right. Perhaps it wouldn't be a good idea to say that to Dad … I've got a better idea – just say, "Dad, Up your B-U-M!"'

'That's the same, isn't it?'

'No, it's not the same at all.'

I have not started to go to school yet, but Dennis has been going for nearly two years, learning to read and to spell. When he says things like B-U-M, that is Spelling. I think I can guess what B-U-M means, and I think Dad can spell too; but is it the same as actually *saying* a rude word?

I walk across the hall to where Dad is standing. He is talking to Mum, standing with his back to me. 'Dad,' I say, 'Up your B-U-M.'

Dad keeps talking to Mum. 'Dad,' – I try again – 'Dad! DAD! UP YOUR B-U-M!'

Dad turns towards me, fast. He turns on one foot, swinging his right arm wide as he spins towards me. It is a single mighty sweep like the swoop of a great bird. His hand is at the furthest end of his wingspan and the hand is moving faster than everything else, and when it comes to rest hard against my buttock its sound is like a thunderclap. A wall of flame spreads out from my B-U-M to my brain, and my admiration of the poetry of Dad's motion gives way to amazement, then to self-pity.

'Dad,' I cry, 'it wasn't my idea!'

I look around for Dennis and, in the far edge of my vision, I catch sight of him retreating, bent double with laughter, disappearing through the door at the far end of the hall.

'Dennis said I should say it to you, Dad! It wasn't my idea.'

When Dad turns to me a second time, the thunder is in his face. He speaks with a terrible intensity and the fire in my buttock is nothing, and the thought of Dad's hand is nothing, and there is only Dad's face and Dad's voice. The voice is speaking: '*Never tell me an untruth, Howard.* Bad words are nothing compared to an untruth. Never tell me an untruth, even if you think it will get you out of trouble.'

I decide straight away that I will never again say anything – true or untrue – in this house. I run outside and leave my home. I will never return. I squeeze myself through the hole in the fence between our place and next door. Here they have started to build a big Catholic church. Here I will find sanctuary. There are piles of bricks and stacks of lumber, as well as great groynes of topsoil thrown up by the builders as they prepared the footings. Between the timbers and the bricks there is good shelter for a runaway. I spend some hours there, among the Catholics, feeling satisfied that my parents have lost their son, and finding comfort watching the builders as they strain and balance barrows full of mortar, pushing them along narrow planks. They never spill a drop.

Eventually the builders stop work and sit down. They light cigarettes and pour hot drinks from thermos flasks and eat sandwiches and thick slices of cake. But to the stranger hiding within their gates they offer nothing.

I decide to give my parents another chance.

Back inside the house, the first person I see is my father. When he speaks this time, his voice is gentle. He says, 'Howard, I want you to make me a promise. I want you to promise that you will always tell me the truth.'

'Dad – I promise. I will never tell you an untruth, ever, in my whole life.'

Now I recall one of Dad's own expressions. It seems to be a good time to use it: '*I give you my word.*'

Dad bends down. His voice is thicker somehow and soft, and his arms hold me close against him. 'That's a good boy …'

'And Daddy,' I continue, 'now that I have promised – it *was* Dennis. Dennis did tell me to say those words to you.'

Daddy leans backwards, away from me a little, searching my face. He looks troubled, then thoughtful. He shakes his head slightly, then says, 'I will look into that …'

❋

Dennis and I have learned how to smoke. It's not easy; you have to light the cigarette with a match then put the cigarette into your mouth and keep it burning. It is easier to light a cigarette if you have someone to help you. I hold the cigarette while Dennis strikes the match and lights it. Then I *blow* air from my mouth through the cigarette to keep the tip glowing red, and when smoke comes out the end, I am smoking. I have to work hard at it. Most people can't do it until they have grown up.

Whenever Mum and Dad have a party they put out ashtrays and lots of cigarettes for their friends. Next morning there are plenty left for Dennis and me. I keep a few and teach a friend how to smoke.

A few days later, Dad steps out of his waiting room into the front yard where I am playing. 'Howard,' he says, 'come with me please.' I follow Dad through the waiting room into his surgery. I am not usually allowed into this part of the house.

'Sit down, Howard.'

Dad sits at the far side of his big desk. There are bright silver doctor's tools in cupboards and on trays, and a very strong smell. Dennis says the smell is ether. Dad gives it to people before he operates on them.

'Howard, I want to talk to you about something very important.' My head feels funny with the strong smell.

'Howard,' Dad's voice comes to me through the ether, 'I want to talk to you about smoking.'

Suddenly my head is clear. My body starts to vibrate. Dad continues: 'Smoking is very bad for you. Patients who smoke come to see me every day with damaged lungs. They cough all the time and they can't breathe. And they want to stop smoking but they can't. It is a habit that they cannot stop … Do you know why I am telling you this, Howard?'

I sit and vibrate and shake my head.

'Howard, I know you have been smoking cigarettes. Mister Saunderson tells me that you have been teaching Jan how to smoke … How old is Jan, Howard?'

'Five, Dad.'

'Jan is too young to smoke …' (I think Dad is right there. She is hopeless at it. Her cigarette keeps going out.) '… and you are too young as well.' Now Dad leans forward and looks at me, into me, looks into my bare soul, and I prepare myself for a second visit from his mighty flying hand. 'Howard, I want you to make a very serious promise. Promise me you won't smoke again until you turn twenty-one. When you're twenty-one you'll be old enough to choose for yourself. I am asking you to give me your word.'

This is easy. 'I promise, Dad.'

Years pass. Voices deepen, hairs grow, armpits smell, and boys in my class start to smoke. My body is thirteen but my mind is older, far too old for this. Boys who would never pick me in their footy team offer me a cigarette; boys who'd never share anything with anyone want to share their smokes with everyone.

I look at the cigarettes and I am not tempted. Groups form of boys who will be men. They joke, they poke and they smoke, but I am not one of them. I gave Dad my word.

In no time I am twenty-one. Prudent as a pensioner, I have passed through my teenage years. My adolescence will have to wait.

Two

Family Ties

When my father was in his late eighties, a public ceremony was held to honour him and two or three other 'Quiet Achievers' in the Jewish community. Dad's friend Jeffrey read the citation, which acknowledged Dad's service to medicine, his contributions to schools and congregations and his unpaid service as a mohel.

As I sat and listened, I looked around me and saw, among the audience of hundreds, faces from his work life, faces from his shule *life, others from his career of quiet leadership in Jewish education, yet others from his work as a* mohel; *and I realised that few of those present had appreciated until now the scope of Dad's contributions to so many fields and over so long a time.*

Over the years, leading pediatricians had spoken confidentially to me about the sad state of ritual circumcision in our community. 'Circumcisions are done so poorly that Jewish men and women, and even doctors, think that mutilation is normal and necessary. When your Dad does a bris, the results are brilliant.'

I looked around the audience and reflected that, as a result of Dad's attentions, men aged from a few weeks to fifty years were better-looking in their undies than their forebears. I visualised a retrospective public exhibition of these well-tempered organs, mounted perhaps by Jewish wives, grateful for Dad's judicious pruning ...

In everything he did, Dad achieved highly and walked humbly.

And now, sitting among the generations of Dad's family, among his friends, his colleagues and scores of his admirers, I swelled with satisfaction.

Then Dad was asked to respond. He shuffled to the microphone, a small figure on the wide stage; he stood there in his unfashionable clothes, a reluctant orator as always. He negotiated with the cordless mike, began to speak, discovered the ON switch, and began again. I noticed that he had no notes.

The speech was short. Dad thanked Jeffrey and the committee, then he thanked the guests. He spoke in the puzzled tone of one who genuinely didn't understand what the fuss was about. He said, 'I wanted always to be worthy, especially of my father and mother … I feared always that I might not be worthy.'

Dad spoke softly. As he spoke of his parents, he searched for the words to express his love and admiration. Even at this great age he placed them on a plane loftier than his own. His concern, his fear that he might be unworthy of them was with him still.

I sat in the body of that hall which was filled with people who had come to do homage to him, and I felt the poignancy of that fear. Here was this estimable, sincere man who had served his fellows so long, and yet he could not rest, could give himself no credit.

I felt sadness for a man who could grant himself no reward, no self-satisfaction. And I felt that I understood my Dad in his fearfulness as keenly as he had felt for me, years before, when I was a teenager sitting in the back of his car.

As I reflect now on the anxiety that shadowed my so competent, confident father, I have the sense that his confidence threatened to unravel in the face of moral disintegration. I mean that Dad showed an unusual intolerance of unreasonable anxiety, of panic in others. Up to a point, Dad would show tenderness and sympathy towards any frightened human being; should fear give way to 'hysteria', however, Dad acted as if he felt threatened. Should another human fall apart utterly, it might shake the very edifice of

Dad's constructed being. Perhaps it was a need to bolster his frail fellows that led Dad into his life as a rescuer.

And in all of these reflections I recognised tremors of fellow feeling.

The stowaway who started it all

The story of the Goldenbergs in Australia starts with my father's father, Joseph. It is the story of a man afloat upon this earth, seeking harbour. Joseph Goldenberg is the grandson of Jews set adrift from Eastern Europe, who settle in an arid colony of the Ottoman Empire, then called Turkish Palestine, but referred to by Jews as the Land of Israel. They settle in Petakh Tikvah, the Gateway of Hope. There, in 1886, my Papa is born within sight of the sand dunes which much later will become Tel Aviv. Over the dunes is the port of Jaffa, the sea, and beyond that, unimaginably distant, lies the British possession of Australia.

Like just about every Jew from an Ashkenazi family, Papa has a grandfather who is a rabbi. As old as Maimonides, Rabbi Moshe Goldenberg's stern face looks wearily out of his faded photograph at his descendants in Australia. I wonder what he makes of us.

If Papa's grandfather were to gaze at his descendants in Petakh Tikvah, he would see only observant Jews. Indeed they cannot imagine any other way to be Jewish.

Papa arrives on these shores in 1898 as a stowaway on a ship from Jaffa. He is twelve years old when he embarks; during the voyage, his bar mitzvah date passes uncelebrated; Papa arrives, a sub-literate boy-man, a foreigner whose only languages are Yiddish and Arabic. Aboard the same ship as Papa is his father, who sails as a legitimate fare-paying passenger.

Papa never tells me the full story of his immigration, so what I record here is a compote of narratives gleaned from my father and from aged aunties who knew Papa longest. My compote is one of a number served in the wider family.

One story suggests that Papa's father sailed to Australia, planning to stay here only long enough to gain British citizenship for himself and his family. This story has it that you could qualify for that status – and gain British consular protection – by residing in Australia for six months.

All agree that Papa avoids all contact with his father during the voyage to save him the cost of his fare; that Papa's father does in fact return to Israel; that Papa stays on in Australia alone. Are Papa and his father in cahoots? Do the two plan the journey together? Does their plan go awry when Papa is discovered and each is forced to deny knowledge of the other? No one knows.

(We do know that Papa's brother leaves home too, and washes up in Dayton, Ohio, where he establishes another branch of the Goldenberg clan. The emotional reunion of the brothers in America takes place decades later, and it enters the folklore of both families. But it is not until ninety years after the brothers' first parting that members of the two branches actively re-enter each others' lives, and the Goldenbergs see themselves again as one clan.)

So my great-grandfather disembarks in Fremantle, and Papa stays aboard ship without word or sign to his father. He leaves the ship at the next port – Adelaide – and makes his way to Ballarat. Papa will not see his father again for twenty years.

Why does a twelve-year-old embark on such an adventure? The stories vary. Dad tells me that Papa loses his mother young, acquiring a classic wicked stepmother who feeds her own children and deprives Papa and her other stepchildren.

Papa himself tells me that he was on the run from the Turkish authorities after he belted an Arab youth over the ear, damaging his hearing. Papa says the youth was older, bigger, a bully who taunt-ed him with *al-yahud!* – the Arabic equivalent of bloody Jew! The colonial police were looking for Papa. They wanted him to assist them with their enquiries.

Perhaps Papa simply wishes to be close to his father, a wish common to fathers and sons who follow. How painful and ironic for both father and son that, in an act of remarkable filial discipline, Papa must be a stranger to his father while aboard, before they part in silence. Father and son might each gaze upon the port of Fremantle, but they must not look at each other.

Family stories say that Papa arrives in Australia with five shillings in his pocket. His educational resources are equally meagre; he has completed only third grade at school, living since then on his wits and his initiative. In Israel, he helped out at the colonial post office in his home town of Petakh Tikvah. Apparently he was a favourite of the postmaster; was there, perhaps, unwelcome affection shown by the postmaster to young Joseph that impelled him to flee? To whom could he turn? What might anyone do?

Before or after the post office job, Papa sold watermelons to fishermen as they return to Jaffa Harbour, tired and thirsty after a day's fishing. Papa describes how he swam out to the incoming boats, floating the melons in the water ahead of him. Competition was keen in the watermelon trade and Papa swam far from shore, trying to be the first watermelon boy to meet the fleet.

As I listen to this story, myself now older than the boy Joseph who braved the deep, I feel certain that my courage would not be equal to the watermelon trade.

This story always strikes me as singular for an additional reason: Papa never swims a stroke in his adopted country. By the time I know Papa, Dad says his father cannot swim to save himself. Does the skill atrophy? Did it ever exist? (I feel, from the circumstantial detail of Papa's story, that it did exist.)

So here is Papa, newly arrived in Australia, on the eve of the Depression, a child (effectively an orphan), unable to speak, read or write English, formerly of the Turkish Postal Service, a retired maritime watermelon trader, a boat person, a persecuted refugee and an illegal immigrant. And an orthodox Jew to boot.

Six years later, he marries in the Ballarat Synagogue. His bride is

Millie (Malka) Grinblat, also formerly of Israel, who has come here as a child with her family on a paid ticket. The Grinblats are poor, but Millie brings a rich dowry to the marriage – a large family, a living, breathing throng of brothers and sisters. For the first time in many years, Papa belongs to an intact family. After years afloat, Papa has made his emotional landfall.

After a few years, the family has moved to Melbourne and Nanny and Papa have three sons. They name the firstborn, Myer. (Earlier, Papa meets a Jewish hawker called Sidney Myer. Papa attends his friend's wedding as an invited guest. Is it after the founder of the Myer Emporium that Joseph names his firstborn?)

Papa is an authoritarian father, patriarchal in religious practice and by temperament. Lacking anything beyond the rudiments of religious learning, lacking a father's guiding hand from an early age, he persists in his observance and succeeds in raising three sons who are devoted in their own religious practice.

Another of the precious photos in our family archive shows Joseph's three sons, gloomily facing the camera. They might be two to five years of age. They wear formal-looking suits of a sombre shade and uncomfortable design. Their rich brown hair is tortured into ringlets. Utterly regimented, comprehensively gentrified, the boys look suitably miserable.

In 1915, North Carlton is a poor suburb peopled by Jews and Italians. Money is tight and Papa is thrifty. He sends Myer to the greengrocers, saying, 'Don't go to the first shop; go to the second one, a mile further along the street. It's a halfpenny cheaper there.'

Papa shops at a cheap grocery in Lygon Street. The grocer asks, 'What can I get you, Mr Goldenberg?'

'Just a pound of flour, a couple of pounds of potatoes and a pint of milk, please, Mr King.'

'What else, Mr Goldenberg?'

'That's all.'

'That's not enough; you've got three growing boys. You need more milk than that, and eggs and butter …'

'I'm buying what I can pay for, Mr King.'

'Here, Mr Goldenberg, you take these eggs and butter, and take another bottle of milk. You take them now. You'll pay me when you can.' From that time, Papa buys only from the grocery owned by Mr King and Mr Godfree.

The years of struggle eventually pass, but Papa never relaxes his frugal ways – except in the curious instance of the musical education of his sons. During the Depression, Papa finds the money to buy a violin for each of the boys and to pay for a private violin teacher. The boys reward their parents for their sacrifice by practising every night in their bedroom upstairs. Downstairs, Nanny and Papa hear the terrible sounds and wonder whether that's the way violin music should be. They are unaware that the boys are sawing away at their fiddles while reading, not sheet music, but comics.

While none of the sons grows up to be a concert violinist, they are all marked, one way or another, by Papa's implacable thrift. Through all the years of my growing up I see how careful Dad is with money. Like his father before him, Dad works hard and sacrifices his own pleasure in order to provide his children with the best available education. When I am fourteen, I manage to win a full scholarship for the final four years of tuition at Mount Scopus College. More than anything I feel relief. Now I can relieve Dad of some strain and expense.

Many, many years later, I learn that the donor of the scholarship ran out of money during my later years at school, and the scholarship was withdrawn. It is not Dad who tells me this. It is Mum, and she tells me only after Dad has died.

'Why didn't Dad tell me at the time, Mum?'

'Because he didn't want you to lose the pride of holding the scholarship, darling. He wanted you to feel you were contributing.'

Papa is not one to lavish praise on his children. Passionate about education, no doubt because of his own lack of opportunity, he serves for years as the honorary Treasurer of the United Jewish Education Board. But he does not confuse academic success with common sense. He says to my father, 'It's a good thing you are a doctor because you'd never make a living at anything else.' Whenever I hear this wild hyperbole I take it for a joke, but Papa does not often joke.

A couple of years after my father passes away, I travel to Israel to honour Clara Goldenberg (her nephews always call her Aunty Claire) who is turning ninety. Assertive, candid, outspoken, she is not cowed by her father-in-law, and in his lifetime I never hear her say anything kind about Papa. But now, in Israel, Aunty Claire astonishes me: 'You know, Papa was a great man. He could have been anything. He should have been a leader, a man in the public eye ... but he was held back by his wife and his family.'

'What do you mean, Aunty?'

'I mean his sense of Nanny's shyness, her timidity. Nanny wasn't emotionally robust. These things shackled him ...'

I am silent, pondering all this. Surely it was Nanny's softness that redeemed their boys. But Claire has another bombshell: '*Papa was always disappointed in all of his children.*' I am speechless. Then indignant. But I have no doubt that his sons would know the true nature of Papa's feelings.

Papa creates a family in Australia that becomes a tribe. The tribe is a cluster of souls, an archipelago of individuals who are Papa's abiding home. His three sons – Myer, Abe and Phil – are colonies, subject from time to time to his small tyrannies. Only one colony ever rises in revolt.

Although it is within this archipelago that Papa lives, it is as if he rides perpetually at anchor. From time to time, he creates a rift from one of his colonies, assuring himself first of the security of his mooring to the other two.

Often Papa indulges himself in an outburst to me against my father. Raising his voice, he delivers himself of his trenchant judgment. Then he collects himself, stops in mid-stream, saying, 'He's your father. I shouldn't speak to you this way ...'

Then he says: *'But he's my son!* I am entitled to say what I think.' Then Papa resumes his tirade and I sit quietly and listen, a submissive island close offshore.

Barry is my youngest brother. As a teenager, Barry is one of the grandchildren least likely to gain Papa's approval. But following Papa's funeral, Barry delivers his judgment of his grandfather. He says to Dad, 'Papa was a great man.' This is a judgment my father has held his whole life through. He is deeply moved now and comforted to hear it from this somewhat unlikely quarter.

It is a valuation of his father that marks *my* father from childhood. It sits upon him like a crown, a crown just too heavy for comfort.

Dad and his brothers

During the Great War against Germany, the name Goldenberg sounds very German to the ears of jingoistic schoolboys in North Carlton. Dad is a shy boy and the hostility he encounters turns him inward. He says he has no friends apart from his brothers but they, with their cousins, are a world. The boys are no strangers to privation; they are proud, and they knit tightly.

Dad is the firstborn, Uncle Abe is the second brother. Phil is the third. When they are small, the older two tell Phil tall and terrifying tales and Phil believes them; because he believes them, the older boys continue to tell frightening stories. Terrified, he clings to his older brothers.

The boys grow and soon the elder two are going to school and learning Australian games such as cricket. They teach Phil how to field and he becomes a permanent backstop while Myer and Abe take turns to bat and bowl. 'Can I bat?' ask Phil.

'Not yet,' is the reply.

'Can I have a turn to bowl?'

'No Phil, you're the fieldsman.'

Phil says he only ever had a chance to bat or bowl after the others had stopped playing and gone inside.

In the synagogue, the three learn the responses and sing the melodies better than most of the adults. They sing at the top of their voices, louder than everyone else and people say, 'That's the Goldenberg boys.' The boys have a single identity.

The Goldenberg boys grow up and marry, but they are still brothers and Dad still looks after the younger ones. The younger two stay in Melbourne, and Dad brings Mum to Leeton. After a while, when Dad needs help with the olives, Uncle Abe leaves Aunty Claire and his small girls in Melbourne and comes to Leeton to help Dad at the farm and in the olive factory. He stays with us a long time, then he goes back to his family.

Every year Uncle Abe comes back for the picking season, and for the crushing and the pickling. He works so hard for his brother – bending, hefting, pushing and pulling – that his stomach ruptures and he needs an operation. He could have an operation in Melbourne, but Uncle Abe wants his brother, Myer, to repair the hernia here in Leeton.

Uncle Phil, too, comes to his older brother in Leeton and stays with us for a while. The grown-ups speak in whispers to each other. Has Something Happened? He plays chess with Mum and talks with her; he rides with Dad in his car on long house calls to patients in Barellan and Yanco and Wamoon. The Something gets better and Phil goes back home to Melbourne.

That threefold cord is not easily broken.

✳

There is a story that passes down the generations into family fable. It is 1995 when I first hear it. Dad recounts it to his newfound cousins at a Goldenberg family reunion in New York. 'Around 1920, my father made his first visit here to see his brother – your grandfather. They hadn't seen each other for twenty-two years. Your grandfather asked Dad, "Have you got a cheque book with you?"

"Of course," said Father.

"Give it to me," said his brother.'

At this point Dad's voice gives way. He struggles with the weight of inherited memory cherished over seventy-five years. The memory of a simple act of loving kindness between brothers undoes my father. When he resumes, his voice is hoarse: 'Your grandfather said to my father, "Give me your cheque book." My father didn't understand. He was uncertain but he handed over his cheque book. Then your grandfather said, "You won't need that while you are here."'

✳

Uncle Abe has two daughters but no sons. He says God didn't give him sons, but we are like sons to him. Dennis and I like this arrangement between God and Uncle Abe, because Abe is the uncle from heaven.

Uncle Abe comes to work in the factory in Belah Street that Dad built to process olives and to improve his tax position. Dad says his tax position has improved out of sight because the Mafia are robbing him at the Queen Victoria Market and the farmer is robbing him on the farm, and if his tax gets any better he'll go broke. Uncle Abe comes to help Dad not to go broke.

Uncle Abe drives a little blue utility truck between Leeton and the farm. The utility is called The Bluebird. It breaks down pretty often, but we like The Bluebird because Uncle Abe gets us to help him to drive. 'Hold the wheel, *boychick!*' he yells. 'Turn to the right, now straighten, now turn left hard! … Thanks, *boychick*, I couldn't do that without your help.'

When we are going along the narrow little track that leads from the made road to the farm, Uncle Abe finds he needs a lot more help with his driving. He picks me up and places me on his knee. 'Grab the wheel, *boychick*, I'm busy with the pedals so you'll have to do all the steering.'

We go along the track and over the grid, through the farm gate, along the track a bit further then around a big bend to the right, before coming to a halt in the shade outside the farmhouse. That adds up to a lot of steering. I have learned how to drive.

'Good driving, *boychick*. Now, take a bit of this ...' Uncle Abe grabs the meat of my thigh in his mighty hand, and applies pressure in the manner of a horse-bite. 'Take that to carry on with.' This sudden compression of all my hamstrings propels me towards The Bluebird's roof. The sensation is intense: part tickle, part squeeze, mainly ecstasy – intolerably good. 'That was just a little something to go on with,' he says, implying that there will be more to follow.

At the farm, I hide behind the car and watch while Uncle Abe bravely faces the farmer who robs my father and talks to him.

On the way back to Leeton we play *gezintas* with Uncle Abe. Dennis is two years older than I and he plays the game better.

'Six *gezinta* thirty-six how many times, Dennis?'

'Six,' says Dennis.

'Good boy,' says Unc.

'Howard, four *gezinta* eight – how many times?'

'Twice, Unc.'

'Good boy, here's a little something to carry on with.'

By the time we get home we have covered the entire multiplication tables – up to ten – in reverse. *Gezintas* are the reverse of multiplication. My thighs are black and blue in token of my arithmetic triumph. In one day I have learned to drive and mastered *gezintas*.

Any old uncle will teach his nephews about farting. But when Uncle Abe lets rip, it is thrilling. He is ahead of his time in decriminalising the act – in private – among consenting males. But when I visit him in Melbourne and lie in the bed he shares with Aunty Claire, I let rip myself, and for the first time he chastises me.

'*Boychick*, I never fart in this bed. I wouldn't do it – out of respect for Aunty Claire. I'd sooner lie here and have a tummy ache than let her feel that I don't respect her.' There is the ring of truth to this lofty claim. Many times have I heard Uncle Abe greet the dawn with ringing farts in his chaste bed in our house in Leeton, while Aunty Claire lies safe in the marital bed in Ellesmere Road, Windsor. Uncle Abe's gentle admonition hits home. I never forget it, and for as long as I live I never again fart in Aunty Claire's bed.

Uncle Abe loves his older brother, Myer, and will do anything he suggests, even to the point of coming with us on Dad's boat. Dad is almost never seasick, and Uncle Abe is invariably sick. Dad invites Abe to come fishing, and he comes along and vomits and lays some berley for Dad, while Dad catches fish. They have a great day. They just love spending time together. That must be the reason he is willing to come to work in Leeton and to sacrifice so much of his life with Aunty Claire and his girls.

Uncle Abe and I first become close on 15 January 1946, the eighth day of my life, when my father bestows upon him the honour of carrying the newborn to Reverend Adler who is about to make his singular spiral mark upon my person in the *bris*. I feel an imperishable closeness to my uncle, the last man to hold me in his arms while I still have a foreskin.

When I am seven years old, I fly unaccompanied to Melbourne in order to experience pain at the hands of an orthodontist who is intent on improving Dad's tax position. I spend the Sabbath – *Shabbat* in Hebrew – with Abe and Clara in Ellesmere Road, and insist on accompanying Uncle Abe on the long walk to Toorak Road Synagogue. The walk is three miles and I am keen to dispel Uncle Abe's misgivings about my stamina, so I set out at a run. I run ahead of Uncle Abe along the small walkway that connects Lewisham Road with The

Avenue. I run as fast as I can and, when my forehead hits the steel barrier designed to stop children running into the path of traffic, it is with considerable surprise that I find myself airborne and horizontal, with those fast legs racing onward still towards The Avenue, while my head and torso are arrested.

In this moment between impact and imminent death, I note how remarkable an experience it is to belt your head so hard. I consider the poignancy of dying young. Then I hear adult footsteps running behind me and in a moment I am in Uncle Abe's arms, I am high in the air, and his face is in mine, and he is almost moaning his question which sounds like a prayer: 'Are you all right, *boychick*?'

In Uncle Abe's arms I am very all right.

✳

The youngest of the three brothers is Uncle Phil. Dad says he is the cleverest. Dad describes with pride how Uncle Phil and a close friend studied Law and Arts at Melbourne University together, and how the two graduated with their twin degrees in the shortest time ever recorded at the University. The friend was called Bob Santamaria.

Uncle Phil is a lawyer in the city, but his true love is scholarship. Eventually he leaves the Law for this truer love. He prepares boys for their bar mitzvah and he teaches Jewish Studies at Mount Scopus, where his name passes into legend among his students.

Towards the end of my secondary schooling, it is Uncle Phil, not Dad, whom I approach for advice about my future. Dad's insistence on literal truthfulness has trained me in the arts of selection and circumlocution, and now I craft my questions to suit my own purposes. Uncle Phil's brain is a razor. It slashes away the undergrowth and overgrowth and lays bare the flesh of my problem. It is terrifying and it is wonderful. It is an education. Uncle Phil teaches me a new word: sophistry.

There must have been a time of confusion in Uncle Phil's early adult life. It arises after his Law studies and before he met Aunty Becky. Dad never speaks of it to me, and none of my aunties recalls it. Only after my father has died do I become aware of it, and then only dimly.

Before his death, Dad charges me to execute his will. He shows me where he keeps his records and his documents. Looking through Dad's desk after his death, I come across an envelope stuffed tight with folded sheets of paper. The paper is cheap wartime stuff; the handwriting is in pencil, in a flowing legible hand. There are three letters, dated over a period of six weeks or so. The letters are from Uncle Phil to my father. The contents astonish me.

Uncle Phil must be in his twenties and Dad would be about thirty. Both are adults, both hold university degrees. Uncle Phil is Dad's junior only in years, yet he humbles himself before his older brother. He writes with a candour and an eager openness of his confusion (unspecified) and his errors (also unspecified). He asks Dad to advise him, to direct his steps, and he – Uncle Phil – will comply. The letters canvas a range of matters – professional, medical, personal and practical – and in all of them, Phil throws himself at the feet of his firstborn brother.

I feel the tremor of filial love projected onto an older brother, as if a father were too daunting a person to approach. As if a good Jewish boy had experimented with a thing undreamed of, as if he had *rebelled*.

Twenty years pass after the writing of those letters. The Uncle Phil I know in 1962 is no one's supplicant. Proud, loud, Papa's equal in the heavyweight wrestling that is Papa's family life, Phil is the independent one in a meshed and knotted bunch of men.

When Dad's parents die we witness Dad and his brothers as they mourn and pay their parents honour. The three brothers spend seven days together in their parents' house. Gentle as an ocean swell, wave after wave of comforters visits the house. In the presence of these old faces the brothers are boys together, sitting and smiling, laughing at the reminiscences brought by relatives and older friends across the sea of years. The brothers defer to each other and speak kindly, sharing the rituals and the prerogatives of mourners. Brotherliness transmutes sorrow; the grieving I see is a kind of joy.

I read and re-read Phil's letters a number of times, but the dark that has gathered I around this correspondence over sixty years remains impenetrable. Dad retained these letters. These three are among the very few that he preserved. He must have seen or handled or passed over this envelope every time he opened that drawer over six decades. When he directed me to the desk as his executor, he must have anticipated that I would one day find the letters. All I can conclude is that a younger brother invested in the older the wisdom and the omniscience of a patriarch and the loving kindness of a saint; and that the older brother cherished those letters for the rest of his life.

Although Uncle Phil is the youngest brother, he is the first of the three to die. A series of medical tragedies starts in childhood when tonsillitis is complicated by rheumatic fever, damaging a heart valve and weakening Phil's heart. In mid-life he develops heart failure, then the surgery to replace the valve results in a stroke, and in a moment that mighty brain is felled. Electric storms come and go within the damaged brain and Phil's last years are marked by pain and dependence.

When Uncle Phil dies Dad mourns but he does not speak his griefs. I have the sense that Dad protects his brother's secrets to the grave and beyond. He leaves to me the legacy of letters that speak of the intimacy he shared with Phil. But of the secrets shared by the brothers, Dad shows no sign and leaves no word.

✴

After Dad dies I receive a phone call from our cousin David, son of Phil. David has lived in Israel these last thirty years. He speaks with love and honour of his Uncle Myer. Then he tells me a story: 'Howard, do you know that our fathers fought over Papa's will after he died?'

This is not how I recall the events; I am at a loss.

David goes on: 'Papa had written his will, leaving his entire estate to the two brothers who were in need – that is, to the younger two. Papa said Myer didn't need his help. Later Papa had second thoughts. He wrote another will, dividing everything into equal thirds. But before he could sign it, he suffered a stroke and lost his speech. He couldn't tell anyone that he'd changed his mind. Papa died without signing the new will.'

As David speaks, I see Papa again in memory, desperately signalling something with two fingers. During those sad, silent weeks, he'd gesture 'two' repeatedly to each of his sons. No one could understand what he was trying to say. He was signalling there are *two* wills!

In my final memory of Papa, he is no longer the domineering patriarch of old, nor the fearsome and austere disciplinarian of my early years; he is an old man in a nursing home, weeping with frustration and grief.

David's voice, on the line from Israel, breaks into my thoughts. 'That's when the argument broke out. My Dad and Uncle Abe came to your Dad and said, "Let's divide the estate three ways, as Father wished."

'But Uncle Myer said, "No. The will stands. I'm the executor. I'll do as Father wrote in his legal will." The other two couldn't persuade your father to accept his share …'

Uncle Abe's two daughters grow up and marry and raise tribes of children and grandchildren in Israel. Uncle Abe and Aunty Claire remain in Melbourne. Abe becomes old and frail. His children beg him to come and settle in Israel, but he stays put. Uncle Phil has passed away and the three brothers are now two. It is only the unbearable thought of parting from his older brother that arrests Abe.

Dad is his still doctor, and the list of ailments lengthens and the ailments worsen and most of them hurt. Uncle Abe's joints were destroyed long ago, spent for his brother in the days of The Bluebird and *gezintas*, in the long seasons of labouring on the farm and in the factory. Uncle Abe has taken the Indocid that his brother-doctor prescribes, every day for forty years. The Indocid pushes up his blood pressure and rots his kidneys.

One of the two boys who were like sons to Abe ministers to him in these years of decline. It is Dennis, his oldest nephew, who is his companion, who fetches and carries for him, who brings this most beloved of men his daily quantum of filial love.

Finally, Abe's kidneys begin to fail. He hears the voice of reason, the voice of his family: *Come to Israel. Don't delay any longer. Come before it's too late. Come now.*

Uncle Abe and Dad realise that this is the time of parting. Dad decides he cannot go to the airport to see his brother fly away. The two boys who were like sons to Abe drive him and Clara to Tullamarine. The sliding doors close, the Jumbo swallows them and they disappear, leaving behind eighty-two years of life and friendship and brotherhood – while Dad sits at home, silent and numb as his brother leaves him at last.

Mystified and terribly hurt, Uncle Abe cannot fathom this first and final desertion by his older brother. In Israel, surrounded by his descending generations, he pens a letter to his brother and gives voice to his desolation. He passes it to Clara to post. Instead she reads the letter and decides that it cannot be sent. Years later she explains: 'It would have hurt your father too much … I loved Myer.'

Abe lives for three idyllic months, then succumbs to kidney failure and dies. My son Raphael is the only Australian resident at his funeral. Back in Melbourne, an earthquake of grief and loss shakes us all.

And my father, the firstborn of three, now twice an amputee, alone survives. He lives on, commanded by an imperious heart and wilful flesh; but the spirit is reduced and is not again made whole.

Sunday wrestling

Dad doesn't have to get up early on Sundays. He lies in bed, relaxing and reading the Sunday papers. It is a good time for getting into Dad's bed for a cuddle. He doesn't get up until it is time to say the morning prayers.

I lie there next to Dad and he puts his arm around me and holds me close to his side. It is peaceful here, and intimate. There are only the two of us and I savour the quiet and closeness. Dad's body is warm. He smells good. After a while Dad says, 'I'd better get up. I need a shave.'

I look at my father. I can't see any whiskers.

'You don't need to shave, Dad.'

'Don't I, Howard?'

Dad rubs his stubbled chin against my cheek. It scratches pleasantly. I want him to do it again and I say, 'I can't feel any whiskers, Dad.' And Dad rubs his chin over my other cheek. The abrading sensation is something like tickling and something like small pain. My face tingles. Dad lies back and resumes reading.

It is summer and Dad's chest is bare. I find myself in the shade of Dad's armpit and consider the view. Under his arm there is a hollow where some brown hairs are growing. On the edge of the armpit is a little mole on a stalk. I wobble it with my finger and Dad jumps and drops the newspaper, saying, 'That tickles, Howard. Stop it.'

I stop it and examine the armpit further. Here is another wobbly mole. I test it with my finger and it is a ticklish one too. Dad jumps in a gratifying manner. The paper falls to the floor and Dad applies his fingertips to my ribs and I discover that I have a few ticklish spots of my own.

Dennis comes in, looking for action. Dad says, 'Boys, just let me relax.' Dennis climbs into bed with us and lies down on the other side to help Dad relax. We all lie still for a few minutes until Dennis reaches over Dad and pokes a finger between my ribs. I jump, the *Sun-Herald* flies everywhere, and Dad draws a deep breath. He looks about him: here is Dennis, his firstborn; there, on the opposite side of the bed is his second son. These are the fruit of his loins.

Dad counts his blessings, but they are insufficient to keep him in bed. He sits up, throws the bedclothes to one side and tries to get up, but he cannot; his firstborn is lying across his legs, pinning them to the bed.

Dad leans forward, seizes one of Dennis' arms and twists it up behind his back. Dennis grunts and lets go of Dad's legs, which Dad now raises forcefully, tipping Dennis off the bed and onto the floor. I leap forward onto Dad, throwing his head back onto the bed to stop him from escaping. Dennis returns to the fray, flinging himself directly across Dad's torso. Margot arrives, small and wiry, followed by Barry, the youngest and smallest, all curly hair and rubber bones.

If Dad were to pause now, he might count one son on his head, another on his chest and two smaller children lying on his legs: four fruits of his loins – a bumper crop. Thus secured at head and foot and in between, Dad will remain our prisoner indefinitely. Dennis says, 'You can relax now, Dad.'

Somehow, Dad does not relax. He thrashes his legs up and down to dislodge his little ones. Margot and Barry hold on for dear life, riding Dad's crazed limbs, up and down until Dad splays his legs and propels two small airborne bodies in opposite directions from his bed.

For the next ten minutes or so, four wild children wrestle with a large, powerful adversary. His strong limbs exercise measured violence against us. He has four limbs, we have sixteen smaller ones. Grinding, straining, struggling, we pit our small muscles against our father's. One by one, he forces us from him, flings us through the air, grapples with the next attacker and the next, in a game of violence that is endless, cyclic, thrilling, hysterical, real and not outlawed by religious statute. We observe the solitary rule: no maiming.

We sweat and we squeal, we experience real pain that is exhilarating; we are busy capturing Dad and ruling him. Our blood is up and nothing can hurt us as we lion cubs fight the king of the jungle. The two smallest cubs are eating carpet when Dad's strong fingers find my ribs and Dennis', and – helpless and hilarious – we fly after Margot and Barry, while Dad rolls free towards the edge of the bed.

Once Dad gets to his feet the game is up. We will have lost him to the world of shaving and seeing patients and saying prayers. Dennis and I will have to go and pray too.

Unaccountably, Dad stalls in his escape. He sits and waits, giving us another chance.

Now all four of us find ourselves astride Dad. He lies face down and breathes hard. The battle is even, the outcome suspended between his stronger muscles and our united force. While we sit upon him and breathe hard, I recall the fable of Aesop that Dad likes to read to us on *Shabbat*, the one about the lion and the three bulls.

At its end, Dad looks up from the book and says with slow emphasis, 'And the moral of the story is: *Unity is Strength*.'

The four young wrestlers grow up and Dad grows old. His parents have long gone and both of his brothers have died. A series of strokes and heart attacks weakens Mum, and Dad's muscles are no longer stronger than ours. Dad becomes frail and ill but he is not ready to accept help. He wrestles alone against Time and against the old Adversary who in the end took away his brothers and most of his patients.

Now his four children conspire to care for him and for Mum. We four doughty individualists once again become a team. Each of us knows better than the others what must be done and how to do it, yet somehow in this endgame we find unity and strength.

Through a year that begins with a vigil and a funeral, followed by seven days of sitting *shiva* – then eleven months of reciting *Kaddish*

— we four, we who always wrestled with our father and who wrestled as strenuously with each other, rediscover an old bond, woven and tested over generations. Again and again, we test its strength. It binds us; we chafe at and see it fray but none of us breaks free of it. Whether a destiny or a lifeline, the fourfold cord persists over the racing years, binding us to those who wove it before us.

Grandfathers

Among the bric-a-brac in my garage there is a heavy steel chest full of relics of my mother's family. It has a curious bolt mechanism, massive steel hinges and snap locks on each side. I imagine it was built to be thief-proof. To lift that trunk when it's full is to risk a hernia.

As well as documents relating to her family going back deep into the nineteenth century, the trunk contains letters written to Mum and by Mum from her teens onward. The items are a curious mixture of dry history (scores of old cheque butts and bank deposit slips for example) and the sentimental.

Fossicking about in the trunk about ten years ago, I find a scrap of drug company notepaper. At its lower margin the drug company advises the doctor:

> When it comes to bronchitis and the inevitable relapse
>
> MOXACIN has the edge

Above this welcome news is a short letter written in a child's hand:

> I love you
> Grandma and
> Grandpa
> Lotsa
> Love
> Rachel
> (Goldenberg)

I read this short epistle and quickly put it back into the trunk. Its contents are painful to me. I don't mention the note to anyone – not to the author, not to the recipients. I nurse the discovery like a secret wound.

✳

As a small child, I address my grandfather as Papa. Very old, older than Time, Papa is whiskery and hot-tempered. He is not patient with small children, and I am frightened of him. Altogether, Papa has nine grandchildren, and he manages to miss out on the sweetness and tenderness of every one of us. Unlike Nanny, who is soft and timid (perhaps she too is afraid of Papa), Papa is displeased by the whole phenomenon of small grandchildren who are imperfect.

Nanny is kind to us. She closes the kitchen door and goes to the far cupboard. From a four gallon tin, she takes a couple of large pastries, studded with raisins. 'These are *zemelach*,' she says. 'Eat them but don't tell Papa I gave them to you.'

From time to time, Dad hears Papa growling at us. At these times he intercedes for us and pleads our case. I feel a sense of rescue and a deep love for a grown-up who remembers how a small child feels.

Eventually, in my late teens, I discover in Papa a man of passion, hot and fiercely loving, a man who wants my love and needs it. Nanny has died and Papa is lonely. I am in matric and I need to study hard for admission to medical school. Papa's house is large and quiet and almost empty. Perhaps it would be useful all-round if I spent a night a week at Papa's place; I could study and Papa would have company.

So it is that every Thursday evening, Papa and I sit in his small kitchen where he used to thunder at small boys, where we drank thin milk for our health and where I would gaze at the worm in the beak of the kookaburra. Papa is grieving, living his lamentation. Jeremiah at the kitchen table, he sits and cries. '*O look and see: is there pain like unto my pain?*'

Papa speaks sadly of Nanny, how he misses her, how beautiful she was.

'Yes, Papa, she was ...'

'What do you know, Howard? You didn't know her when she was younger ... Before you were born, when she was younger, she had a fine figure' (at this stage the conversation is becoming uncomfortable, but Papa presses on) 'and she had full, firm breasts ...' (now I want to run, run away from this candour, run from Papa's palpable grief).

Thursday after Thursday, Papa grieves and I listen in the kitchen, then we go to the 'breakfast room' – that's what Nanny and Papa always called it, though I never saw anyone eat breakfast there – and in the breakfast room, Papa consoles himself with an evening of television. Dutiful, attentive, and lacking a TV set in my own home, I console Papa every Thursday night in the breakfast room until the close of transmission. Then I go upstairs and try to study Optics, falling asleep over my textbook. By the end of matric I have a very good knowledge of Eliot Ness and 'The Untouchables', and an indifferent knowledge of Optics.

And I have come to know my grandfather and his love.

※

My daughter Rachel is the firstborn grandchild of both of her sets of grandparents. Her maternal grandparents take to their new vocation with relish. They become Nana and Zeide. They love their new status and they set about adoring Rachel, being quickly adored in return. They seem to lack all critical sense: they can see no fault, and hotly deny any assertion of fault in Rachel and in the further five grandchildren who tumble after her into their lives.

Nana and Zeide find plenty of time for their grandchildren. (So does my Mum, who is called variously, Grandma or Bom, the latter being an ancient and loving family name created by a toddler who could not say Yvonne.)

But Dad is too busy. Dad is a doctor and he must care for his practice. With Rachel's arrival in 1972, Dad becomes a grandfather. He is sixty-two years old, and for the next thirty years he is too busy looking after patients to have much time for grandchildren. And when he finds himself in their company, he has forgotten how he used to intercede for his own imperfect children. He feels grumpy and he shows it.

Rachel is a firstborn. (Like her paternal grandfather before her, and like his father before him, Rachel must contend with inexperienced parents who grope and stumble their way into parenthood.) As a toddler, Rachel grizzles, contests, raises her voice in unseemly protest and tries to manipulate her parents, often enough succeeding. All of this my father sees and registers – and he does not like it. A child does not raise a voice to a parent; that was the rule he was raised with, and that is the rule he raised me with. It is a rule I am happy to observe but unwilling to impose.

So Rachel becomes a granddaughter who Does Not Honour her Father and her Mother, a cardinal precept, particularly as regards a father. My father seems to have lost the memory of what it is like to be a small child.

Years pass. I have conversations with Dad in which I try to share with him the glow, the joy of being Rachel's father. But all Dad can see is the child whose disrespect is hurting his son. I want Dad to love her but, if he cannot, at least to enjoy my love of her. But he cannot do this either. I want Rachel to love my father, but I cannot hope that such love will take root in a stony soil.

Rachel becomes a teenager and begins to map out her path in life, and the path is not that of Orthodox Jewish observance. Now Dad is pained beyond words for my disappointment. He cannot forgive Rachel for her treatment of me. Dad cannot see, cannot hear how greatly Rachel gives me just that joy that he would wish me from a child of mine.

After a time, I try not to introduce mention of Rachel into our conversation. Smouldering with judgment, Dad preserves a tactful silence. He wants to protect me.

After finishing secondary school, Rachel goes to Israel to study. She enrols at the Hebrew University on Mount Scopus, and there she settles into her studies. She becomes interested in Pablo, a student from Argentina. Soon Rachel is majoring in Pablo and Rachel becomes Pablo's curriculum in turn.

Over the next few years, Rachel shares her time between Australia – where she pursues a desultory Arts degree – and Israel, where she works to support herself, and where she and Pablo continue their pursuit of each other. This pursuit is not desultory.

Neither Rachel nor Pablo is religiously observant. The couple share a house. I do not ask any questions and I feel no need to. I am satisfied that they care for each other deeply. I report the bare bones to my father. I tell Dad, 'It's a battle to live on fragments of income in an expensive city like Jerusalem. I want to give Rachel some material support. On the other hand, I don't want to signify that I support everything she is doing. So I send her money to spend on making *Shabbat* a special day.'

As I speak, the voice I hear sounds uncomfortably like the voice of a manipulative religious father trapping his secular daughter in a life she has rejected. But neither Rachel nor Dad feels that way; united at least in their love of me, they see only the kindness in my actions.

Dad says (not for the first time), 'Howard, you are a far better father than I have been, far wiser …'

I cannot square this with my own experience.

After some years, Pablo joins Rachel in Australia and the couple marry. Immediately following the ceremony under the *chuppah*, I look up and here is Dad approaching me, arms outstretched. We fall into each other arms, clasp hard, our bodies and our faces locked. Neither of us speaks, neither lets go. We hold and we both know everything the other is feeling. We have never loved each other more. We have never been closer than we are in these long wordless minutes.

Rachel is twenty-four and Dad is eighty-six when I first go to the garage and find that old steel trunk. I lock the note away and manage not to think about it until ten years later, when Rachel is a mother three times over, and my father is dead.

When I return to the trunk, hernia-hoist it and lug it inside, the note is far from my mind. I am looking for scraps of old family history but there, nestling among ancient wedding certificates and letters that Dennis and I wrote to Mum when we were small, is the scrap of notepaper upon which Rachel, aged nine, indites her hopeful love. A loving grandmother must have declared it a treasure and locked it away.

I open the notepaper and read the words. More precisely, I misread them.

> I love you
> Grandma and
> Grandma
> Lotsa
> Love
> Rachel
> (Goldenberg)

The ragged handwriting has the melting effect of a child's face in slumber. The unevenness of the lettering, the chirpy Hello Kitty cool of 'lotsa love' melts me in reminiscence. When finally I read it as it is written, when I realise that a letter Rachel plainly intends for both grandparents actually *excludes* mention of 'Grandpa', I smile wryly at the inadvertence of our acts and the accidents that make up our histories.

I cannot hold that note without smiling fondly at the child she once was. At the child I was. At the child that each of us remains. I read it again and the feelings are as keen as ever, but sorrow loses its keen edge and mellows into regret for Dad and Rachel. Unlike my Papa and me, they never knew each other.

Three

At Sea

My father loved the sea. From his boyhood, when he and his brothers rowed their own father in a longboat to the fishing grounds of his arbitrary choosing, until the end of his long life, my father was happiest on the water. It was on the water that I saw my father at his most relaxed … and at his most intense.

Dad used to tell a story against himself from his land-bound years in Britain. Starved of recreation afloat, Dad hired a sailing boat on the Serpentine in London. It was mid-winter, and Dad was rugged up in a greatcoat and a bowler hat. He set off from the pier, sailed across the lake and, in turning, misjudged the wind. The small boat capsized, upending Dad into the lake. He surfaced, wet and cold. He saw his bowler floating away from him on the surface of the Serpentine. He abandoned ship and struck out across the lake to rescue his hat!

My father knew that boating and all water sports are conducted in an alien element, where life hangs upon misjudgment. Here, my father's many gifts and abiding anxieties were always at play. Here, in a theatre of unforgiving reality, my father taught his children inescapable truths.

Death by water

It is a boiling hot day in Leeton. Later, we will go down to the river for a picnic with our friends. Even though it is already quite hot, we aren't ready to go; we are waiting for Dad. As it is Sunday, Dad doesn't have any regular work to do, so he'll 'just see one or two patients' at the hospital, then we'll all go together.

We wait at home, where the flat tin roof warms the house up nicely. We wait just one or two hours beyond Dad's expected return. Lunchtime comes, the picnic is packed and ready and we are still here, waiting. Then Dad phones from the hospital and tells Mum to drive down to the river without him. He'll follow soon and meet us at Eurolie Beach.

But we can't all fit in Mum's car, so John Morrison and I stay behind. He and I sit in the curtained dark of the sweltering house and, quite soon, Dad arrives.

He changes into his black bathing costume, but instead of jumping straight into the car, he says, 'I'm too hot to drive just yet. Let's have something cooling first.' He dives under the kitchen table, where he reaches into a wooden crate and emerges with something dark green and large in his hands. It's a watermelon. It's so big that Dad has to use two hands to heave it onto the table. I never suspected there was this secret melon cache. Who else knows?

Dad takes a great big knife from the kitchen drawer and cuts three large chunks of dripping red melon that bleed juice all over our bare tummies. As we sit wordlessly on the cool stone floor, we suck and chew and slurp all that sweetness in a feast which is ours alone. My chunk is so thick that I am not sure at first how I'll get it into my mouth, but I manage.

Those unlucky ones down at the river won't know what they are missing. We three men sit and consume slice after slice. Only after we have finished the monster off do we drive down to the beach, bursting with secret pleasure.

John Morrison is a handsome man, younger than Mum and Dad.

He wears his shiny hair brushed back. He is the bachelor brother of Jessie Harris, our friend. Now that he and Dad and I have feasted together on melon, we are friends.

❋

It is another hot day in Leeton. The Harris and Goldenberg families gather at the Hay Canal. As usual, we are going to sail Dad and Jack's little yacht on the swift waters of the canal. The boat is a Vaucluse Junior, also called a 'VJ'. Dad built it with his own hands.

I know about this canal; I have watched Dad aquaplaning on it, and we have all sailed here, often. Every time we come here, Dad says, 'This canal flows for ninety miles, all the way to Hay.' It sounds like a warning.

I have swum here too, swimming my few frantic strokes, always within grabbing distance of the bank, aware of the strong current that would overcome a body and carry it downstream, all the way to Hay.

Mum and I stand on the bank and watch the VJ as it tacks up and down the canal. Dad, my older brother, Dennis, and John are aboard. Dad gives Dennis a go at the tiller. Dennis is eight years old and good at steering. After a while, the bow runs between the grasses on the opposite bank and the boat is caught in the shallows. John steps up from the cockpit onto the foredeck to push off into the stream. He grips the steel forestay to steady himself, and pushes the bank with one foot. As he steps forward, the little boat lifts and sways, its mast strikes the powerlines above and John falls, falls without a cry into the water.

Now Dad and Dennis are alone in the boat, and the boat is moving backwards in the current. Dad half rises, leans over the gunwhale and, peering into the water, makes to dive. He then looks behind him at Dennis in the cockpit, and sits down again. Trapped between the current and the deep, Dad points and shouts, shouts with a mighty voice, a roar from Wamoon to Leeton.

There are answering shouts from the bank … adult faces gaze anxiously towards the yacht … adult feet pound along the bank in our direction … Jack Harris is running, racing towards us. Jack, a giant of a man, is running, running with his big tummy and in bare feet. I've never seen Jack run before.

I turn to Mum. 'Why is Mister Harris running? Why is he diving into the water like that? Why is he swimming underwater? Why doesn't he come up?'

Mum has her back to me. She is looking at the water. When she answers she hasn't turned. Her voice comes from a distance: 'Jack is worried …'

Mum breaks off as Jack surfaces and gasps: 'I had him, I had his hand!' Then Jack dives again and Dad is suddenly there, and he dives too.

Moments later, Dad and Jack are pulling a white body from the water onto the bank near us. More shouting: 'Get the truck, quick!'

As Mum leads me swiftly away from the men, I see Dad bending over the body, performing the elaborate rituals of artificial respiration, semaphoring John's limp limbs to drain the water from his chest and to suck air into him.

In no time Jack's truck arrives, Jack and Dad lift John onto the tray, then Dad resumes his work as Jack leaps behind the wheel and the truck surges and roars past us, racing along the track and over the bridge before turning towards Leeton and the hospital. Dad bends and continues the forlorn ballet of resuscitating John, aboard the bucking tray of the speeding truck.

That evening, Mum says, 'They've put John into the iron lung to make him breathe.'

Later we are at the table eating tea, when Dad comes home. He says, 'John has died. The iron lung didn't save him.'

He was electrocuted. Electricity from the powerlines ran down the metal stay that he was holding and through his body, and into the earth where he rested his foot.

Dad sits down heavily. After a while he says, 'Dennis darling, it wasn't your fault. It was an accident. It wasn't anyone's fault. We never thought … I couldn't save him …' He stops speaking and nobody says anything.

Dad and Jack sell the VJ and we never again go sailing on the canal.

My father the sailor

It is night. The boat rises and falls on the swell as we load it in the darkness. The light at the end of the jetty shines on the black water that rises towards a small boy and subsides, mesmerising him. The boy is prone to periods of 'absence'. The father says he is a dreamer. Oil droplets on the water are like rainbows on the face of the deep. The jetty light shines upon the white decks of the boat, and beyond this brilliance the night seems darker and the water blacker.

Dad's voice calls and the boy that was me says, 'OK,' and resumes loading. Pillows, sleeping bags, boxes of canned food, jerrycans of petrol, cakes baked by Mum, cheese, bread, and navigation charts – all are taken below into the cabin. We also bring aboard the things we wear when saying our prayers – *tallith* and *tefillin* – as well as Dad's medical bag. Everything is stowed in the cabin where we four children will sleep while Dad steers the boat to the far end of Port Phillip Bay.

Inside the cabin a thin light is cast by a small overhead globe. We use this light sparingly. You are not supposed to run the light for too long in case you flatten the boat's batteries.

We stow everything that will fit in lockers. Bigger items are wedged firmly against each other on the floor. Dad wants everything shipshape before we set out for Queenscliff. Things are shipshape when they won't fall or spill or break or crash when our boat gets thrown around in the sea.

We get into our sleeping bags and lie down on our bunks – all four of us children, and Dad too. He will sleep until midnight then awaken to cast off and navigate through the dark, all the way to Queenscliff. Dad prefers to go by night, to find his way by chart and compass, and by navigational markers like the South Channel Light.

Dad is a real seaman. He stands alone in the dark on the afterdeck while we sleep below. He never wears a lifejacket. What would happen if Dad were to fall off the back of the boat while it is under way and we are sleeping below? Who knows? None of us has considered this eventuality, which would seem to us children as improbable as a mermaid taking the wheel.

The water laps its lullaby against the timbers of the boat; I turn onto my side on a bunk that is so narrow, you couldn't have a decent erection. I say my prayers, warm up my sleeping bag with a few sweet farts, then fall fast asleep.

A roar followed by a throbbing batters against the walls of my dreams as Dad casts off and the motor powers the boat away from the jetty towards the open sea. Here the swell is larger and the boat climbs and slides its way southwards while I try to stay asleep.

I don't want to wake up in case Dad presses me into service on deck. It can be fun steering the boat and trying to keep it on course, but not when it's dark and cold and wet up on deck. When the wind howls and the boat rocks I want to be in my bag on a bunk while Dad keeps watch above.

The Bay is treacherous. Conditions can change abruptly, and often do so. A silent passage across a millpond can erupt into a heaving, foaming, tossing plunge through air and water. Dad says Port Phillip is as dangerous a stretch of water of its size as any in the world.

What is more, ours is a motor boat. It has only one motor, a Chrysler Marine engine which often breaks down. There is no auxiliary mast for sails. We don't have a two-way radio aboard, so if the engine conks out, you can't call for kerbside help. There is only Dad to fix it.

Sometimes the engine fails and the weather turns nasty at the same time. At these times I see my father's face looking serious and determined. I realise that Dad is all that stands between us and some terrible event. His face is grim.

These are the times when I wish my Dad were not so able and self-reliant. And a person who is a bit of a dreamer by day might prefer it if he were dreaming on his bunk below decks, now. Without warning, my sleep is interrupted for a second time; a change has taken place. The motor, a huge inboard beast which has throbbed at my side for hours, is coughing and firing by turns. Cough, cough, cough. Then silence. Have we arrived? I sit up and look out through the window. I see in the light of early morning – not Queenscliff, but sea – an endless, lumpy sea of leaden green, upon which small white tops are breaking at an angle to the swell. There are darkening clouds and a rising wind. This is what Dad calls dirty weather.

The boat starts to roll noisily from side to side. Things that should have been shipshape now leap and crash about. Quickly, I lie down again and close my eyes.

Dad is inside the cabin, kneeling on the floor and removing the heavy wooden casing that houses the engine. He pulls a piece of greasy tubing free of its attachment to some more tubing, then sucks hard. Somehow he avoids getting a mouthful of the petrol that flows in response to his sucking. He restores the tube to its attachment and goes aft where he turns a key. The starter motor shrieks inside the cabin, then groans and subsides. Nothing happens. Dad tries again and again. The whinnying and groaning inside a rolling cabin which now smells richly of spilled fuel, are not pleasant.

In my bunk I concentrate on the sounds that I hear. Repeatedly, Dad tries to start the motor. The screams lengthen as Dad holds the key turned, but that half groan follows, then that ugly silence falls. I hold my breath.

Another turn of the starter motor, another non-start of the engine, then a new sound – Dad is using Strong Language: 'Damn and Blast!' Another try, a further failure, an intensifying of the language of a mechanic who is at sea: 'YOU BITCH!'

Once again Dad is inside the cabin, kneeling and sucking. The boat rolls harder. It rolls over so far that it must capsize, then it steadies and rolls back, and Dad's knees lose their purchase on the floorboards. He lurches and his head smacks against the hard metal of the Chrysler Marine engine. 'You bitch!' says Dad again, and pays no attention to his cut forehead which starts to bleed. He takes another suck, petrol flows up the tube and into his mouth. He spits, then vomits into the bilge. He gets up and moves quickly aft, where he turns the key. The starter motor produces a sustained, battery-draining cry of agony, the motor roars an enraged response, Dad shifts the gear lever and the boat surges forward. Dad leans on the tiller and we turn south again and head for Queenscliff.

I decide not to stay inside with the petrol fumes and the open bilge that surges with Dad's thin vomit. I find a bandaid and move aft.

'Do you want me to steer Dad?'

※

Another trip. We are singing. All of us kids are up on deck with Dad in the brilliant sunshine, holding on hard as the boat rides the waves.

> A capital ship for an ocean trip
> Was the *Walloping Window Blind*.
> No wind that blew dismayed her crew
> Or troubled the captain's mind.

We sing at the top of our voices, trying to hear ourselves over the roar of the engine which is also in pretty good voice this morning. We are heading for open water where we will drift for flathead. Flathead are deservedly known as the most stupid of God's creatures: any fool can catch them (which explains my success) but the success feels empty. They are only good eating if you like bones. And once you have caught one, you have to remove the flathead from the hook. During this process the fish shows its ingratitude towards you by thrashing about, frequently impaling your finger on one of its numerous barbs. Now it is your turn to thrash about in pain, until Dad says, 'Rub your finger in the mucus on a flathead's belly.' This suggestion has as much appeal as poking your finger up the nose of a stranger who has a bad cold, but it does stop the pain.

We are singing the chorus as the boat rides and plunges over the oncoming sea, casting a drenching spray over anyone sheltering aft in the cockpit.

> Then blow ye winds, heigh-ho
> A-roving we will go
> I'm off to my wife
> With the carving knife
> Ten thousand miles away.

Mum is lying down below in the cabin, reading. This is a weakness and a folly in Dad's eyes. For Dad, action is virtue – whether at work or on holiday. For Mum, a cabin empty of her five jolly sailor boys and a good book are bliss.

Dad knows how to overcome bliss. He cajoles Mum to come up on deck: 'You'll enjoy the sunshine, Yvonne.' Mum complies, the boat leaps and smacks into an oncoming wave and Mum gets drenched as she emerges from the cabin. Having enjoyed the sunshine Mum goes inside and dries off and resumes reading.

Dad cuts the motor. We begin to drift for flathead, the boat goes side-on to the waves and begins to roll. The sun goes behind a cloud, the wind whips my nipples and I retire below, shunning virtue for a good book.

Almost immediately, there is a slapping on the deck above my head. Dad has landed a flathead, a big one by the sound of him, doing its death dance and summoning the hunter below. Moments later Margot – she is one of us jolly sailor boys – and Dennis and

Barry are landing flathead too. But the hunter below is in the jungles of Africa, where a lion has crept downwind of Tarzan and has sprung towards him as he bends forward to drink from a stream.

Up on deck, the wind is doing its mischief with the fishing lines. Tangles are developing. The death dance of many fishes becomes a corroboree. Everywhere, fish flail about on deck, tangling further those fine filaments of line.

'Mum! Mum! Can you come and help me with my tangle?' The cry from the throat of one or more of her children penetrates Mum's reverie. Here comes the wife with the carving knife, says she, as she makes the deck and sits down for a labour which will not end until we return to port.

'Come and fish, Howard, the flathead are on the bite!'

But Dad's summons goes unheard. Tarzan and the lion are wrestling in a life and death struggle.

Somehow, some time, the motor starts, the boat is under way, and Mum has come inside to avoid the dampening effects of sunshine. Tarzan has a half-nelson on the lion and is engaged in a mighty effort of muscle to break the beast's neck.

There is singing overhead:

> And the cook was Dutch
> And behaved as such ...

The magnificent muscles at the back of Tarzan's neck are bunched and contracted. He forces the lion's neck further forward with his laced fingers. A breathless moment, a snapping sound is heard, and the great creature falls dead at Tarzan's feet.

The motor has stopped and somehow the boat has not begun to roll. I go up on deck and discover that we have tied up in Pope's Eye, one of the loveliest spots on Port Phillip Bay. According to Dad, The Pope's Eye is an annulus, an incomplete circle of rocks which face The Rip. There used to be cannon mounted here, aimed towards the entrance to the Bay, where the invading Russians would have to pass on their way to Melbourne. If only Melbourne were to fall, the Russian Bear would have a strategic stranglehold upon the world: Minsk, Pinsk and Moonee Ponds tightening an irresistible pincer grip on the world's arteries.

In the event, we scared the Russians away and took down the guns. A century too soon, in my opinion, as we face the Russians once again, in Berlin and in Budapest, and fear them everywhere.

We have tied up in the annulus, not for its scenic beauty but for its shallow depth and its shelter. The engine is overheating and will soon seize up unless Dad can fix it.

Dad reckons there must be something choking the water inlet which sucks sea water into the boat to cool the motor. Dad is holding onto the rail and leaning over the side, peering at the inlet. But he can't get a good view because the inlet is below the water line.

Dad calls for help. 'Who wants to dive over the side and unblock the intake?' I do. That is, I think I do – until I contemplate our proximity to the open ocean, to Tasmania and, beyond that, to Antarctica.

In my moment of irresolution Dennis helps me by pushing me firmly in the small of my back. I descend, swim under water to the hole in the hull, and find a plastic bag blocking the intake. I yank it out and surface to a hero's welcome. Dad starts the motor and it's:

> Blow ye winds yo ho
> A roving we do go
> And Dennis will pay
> Yes he will pay
> He'll rue this day
> I'll have my way …

Dennis doesn't have to wait long. At bedtime he finds a cold, dead flathead awaiting him in the bottom of his sleeping bag. Treading on a flathead is like putting your toes up someone's runny nose. And there's always the chance of a nasty sting.

There are all sorts of songs you can sing in a boat. With the boat speeding across the water, and the four of us kids up on deck with Dad, and the wake all white in parallel lines behind us, and the morning sun brilliant on the water and thawing our cold-tight skin, you sing for warmth and you sing for joy and beauty and for being together. Sea songs are called sea shanties. Dad says it comes from the French word for singing. Like the great arias of opera, ours are all songs of love and death.

Our boat is old and unreliable and unfashionable. But it's big and comfortable and it sleeps six on its narrow bunks. There is a big table and a small and smelly toilet. You go into that toilet and stand there and watch the sea water rising and falling in the bowl with the motion of the boat. It can distract you from the business at hand and from your aim. Sometimes you go in and have to sit down, and the boat moves up and down and you have visions of the cold sea rising in the bowl and kissing your warm bottom.

We are the only Jewish family among the families that gather with our boats each year in Queenscliff, but we feel at home here. Dad has been coming here since he was a little boy. He grew up with the kids of the fishing families, and his father – my Papa – used to fish with the professionals here. Dad is proud of his father's skill. He says the fishermen liked to take Papa fishing with them because he'd increase their catch.

The fishing families around here don't find our Jewishness strange; they've known us now for three generations and we are comfortable together. Olga and Roy have known Dad and his brothers all their lives. They come and eat a meal with us on board our boat. Roy sits at our big table and picks up his fried flathead in his short fingers. Some of his fingers are missing, and he doesn't use a knife and fork. I watch, fascinated. Did a great fish take those fingers?

We meet old Alby who tells us about the times he's been shipwrecked. He's seventy and he's never learned to swim. He just hung on to some floating timber from his wrecked shark boat until someone came and rescued him. It was two days and a night before they found him. He tells us this and just laughs, his great pink face all burned and scarred by seventy years of sun and sea. You would not know, from his face of smiles, of the people he has known and lost.

Maureen is Alby's daughter. She is Mum's age, and she has a red-headed daughter but no husband. Nobody talks about this; did he drown in a shipwreck? Maureen and Little Red live with Alby and Maureen's brother, Murray, who looks after them. Murray and another fisherman are going to take us out floundering when the moon and the tide are right, but when the night comes with the right tide and the right moon, we don't go because (as Dad explains) the fisherman is very tired. So are we all – we have waited up past midnight. So we go to bed. In the morning we learn that the fisherman had been in the hotel all the afternoon and all the evening and had become so tired he couldn't stand up straight.

Most of the people at the yacht club drink a lot of beer. Dad doesn't drink much but people make allowances because he is a doctor, which is different. Is it because Dad is a doctor that people at the club don't mind us being Jewish? The Greek man on the boat at the far end of the jetty is short and round, and he smokes a cigar and laughs a laugh that is fathoms deep. His boat, like ours, is old and unfashionable. Although he is a man, he likes to cook and you can smell the garlic and the olive oil when he is cooking. He is not a doctor, and he is rather Greek, so the yacht club is glad that he keeps his boat and his smells at the far end.

We are not the only people at the club who sing. In the long evenings, as we lie on our bunks and the other boat people keep on drinking, we hear the adults singing loudly. They sing and they laugh and their voices are loud across the water. If you look through the portholes you can see their faces, red in the lamplight. Sometimes you hear water splashing on water, and you see one of the men holding onto a bollard and peeing from the jetty. You fall asleep to the sounds of their laughing and singing.

As well as our large motor boat we have a sailing dinghy. Dad teaches us to sail it. He shows us how to hoist the sail, how to turn the boat without tipping it over and how to get the boat back upright if it does tip over. He knows all these things. He teaches us how to have fun on the water and to be safe.

Because you can die on the water. Dad never forgets John Morrison, handsome John, dying young on the water. It was another boat in another time.

We sail and we have fun and Dad makes sure we are safe. He doesn't say anything about John Morrison or the little boat on the Hay Canal. But he's very fussy about safety.

When the day has died Dad sings a lullaby:

> Sweet and low, sweet and low
> Wind of the western sea,
> Low low, breathe and blow ....
> While my little ones,
> While my pretty ones sleep.

✳

'Howard – grab a lifejacket and come up on deck – quickly!'

I have been lying on my bunk, reading, hoping to stay below decks and read out the storm. Dad and I have long agreed that I am an idiot. He points it out whenever I carry out any practical task. He tells me how to do the task before I do it, then while I'm doing it, then after I finish.

Dad knows the only right way and I create a variety of wrong ways. Dad points out these errors as consistently as I make them.

A rough passage from Portarlington to Queenscliff calls for a non-idiot, a practical person, not to mention a brave one. And Dad is very brave. With Dad up on deck a storm feels manageable, just another fight against the elements. The boat can leap and crash and roll; Dad can hold his own.

If Dad needs help, there are likelier candidates. I have an older brother – but he's away at camp – and I have an older mother, if it comes to that. But Mum suffers from being a woman, so she isn't logical. I know about women and logic because I hear Dad telling Mum, quite frequently.

So this summons to the arena of heroes is unusual. I do not relish this new opportunity to be an idiot. I put on a lifejacket and a brave face – brave but not, I hope, heroic.

Up on deck I discover that this is not a storm; this is something different. The wind screams. Dad shouts something but the wind snatches his voice away. I come closer, bracing by hand and foot, and Dad's mouth is in my ear as the boat convulses in the tortured sea.

'Howard, I need you to go up forrard. Tell me if you see land and where you see it. You'll have to hold on tight. And put on a waterproof – it's going to be wet.'

I look up. Ahead of the boat there is no sky. There is no sea either. The wind is whipping everything into a white foam. The world is bleached and wild and very beautiful.

Dad said he needs me up forrard: *me!*

Down below again, I decide to take off everything except my bathing togs and the lifejacket. I put a waterproof on over the jacket and go back on deck, where a fusillade of horizontal rain stings my eyes.

More ear-to-mouth megaphone: 'Howard – we have to keep away from the shore. We're about to pass the Point George Light and then we want to go in a straight line towards the West Channel Light. If we go inshore of that line we could hit Governor's Reef. This squall is blowing us towards the land across the reef. I need you to keep a lookout; tell me when you see the Point George Light. It should come up soon.

'And Howard – one more thing: there is a second light which

flashes every 6.75 seconds – when you see that white light you know we've got plenty of depth – we're in safe water. But if you see the light flashing red, we're too far inshore. We might be near the reef.'

I inch my way forward. My bare feet are bathed in turn by the warm water of the waves that crash over the bow, and the colder water of the rain that pelts still, smiting me from top to toe. The boat is drunk, a maniac that tries to hurl me overboard as it thrashes against the seas. Abruptly the engine falls quieter and the boat ceases its leaping. Dad has throttled back to allow me an easier passage along the deck to the bow.

I turn and wave, screaming, 'Thanks, Dad!'

Dad said the light I want flashes white. I scan the waters in front of me for a white light. But everything is white – the rain and the foam and the seas ahead. The white dances against the near-white and the grey-white, but no light flashes.

Gripping the stout front rail I lean forward, peering for a glimpse of the signal of safety or of danger. Dad has revved the engine again to make sure we do not lose steerage way. As we leap and dive through the waves I begin to wonder how strong is the *Margot Carolin*. Dad says she's strong enough for anything that Port Phillip can throw at her. And I know she won't sink because she's built of wood and Dad says wood is lighter than water. That's good because there's water everywhere; it's up to my knees now, then suddenly it has gone as the bow rides high over an engulfing wave.

But no boat is safe if it crashes onto rocks, and Governor's Reef is a line of rocks just below the waterline. Unseen, they wait for craft that come their way, then gouge their bottoms like waiting sharks. They eat wooden boats like ours for breakfast. I know because Dad told me.

I am up forrard and Dad is a few feet away at the wheel. Everyone else is below. Dad steers and runs the engine and I keep a look out across the water with eyes that fill and sting with the waters of the squall. We are the only two people in the world. We are the two people who are keeping the others safe.

Something black and big is in the water, just ahead and to starboard. I yell and wave and point at the huge black form. As I hold on and pivot and look towards Dad, a wave washes my feet from beneath me and I land on my bum on the deck. But I am still holding on, holding on and looking towards Dad. And Dad is waving back and nodding and flashing me a grin.

I look up at the black thing and see a flash of white from the light at its top. We are passing the Point George Light, surging past, passing from safety towards the Governor's Reef.

I look ahead into the white for a white light. I look anxiously to starboard for sight of white sand. I look at the walls of white and the falling showers of white and the rain pellets of white in a world that dances about me. The deck that dances beneath my feet is painted white. I turn and look at Dad. His navy beanie is a black mush. Mine must look the same. In a world of white and wet, only Dad and I have form and colour.

The only sounds are the crash and splash of water, the howl of wind from the end of the world; and behind these, the baritone drone of a marine engine. The howling world is empty of speech. I move and brace, ducking waves as they break over us to stay upright, Dad sways as he steers and peers below at his instruments and above at the whiteness. We are in a dream, serene in a world of mime, a ballet. My Dad and I are two mortals alone, struggling on an epileptic sea. One captain, one deckhand – no idiots.

It is a time which has no measure. It comes to an end when suddenly the white lifts, the wind drops, the sun – unruly old fool – bursts in upon our intimacy. The squall has come and it has passed. There, far away to starboard, is the creamy yellow of St Leonards sandy beach. And here, straight ahead, is the West Channel Light. It flashes at me every 6.75 seconds, flashing white, winking and saying welcome, well done, you are safe. You two have brought your family safe and sound, far from the Governor's Reef.

I turn to Dad and point at the light. He smiles. His voice is a new sound in a new world: 'Thank you, Howard. Well done.'

The helmsman

There is an unfamiliar boat moored at the yacht club jetty. Large and elegant, it has white decks that gleam in the summer sunshine. It floats gracefully on the slow swell as the sun dances over the water. The boat is one with the water and the melting sky. It is a seabird with white wings. It moves languidly, a hovering pelican.

The beautiful boat draws us close. Tommy, my schoolmate, and I sit on the edge of the jetty, our legs dangling over the side. Half a metre away, the boat rises and falls with the rhythm of the sea.

'Don't hang your legs over the jetty!'

The voice has an edge, urgent, absolute. The voice is Dad's, the voice of command, of commandment, of *thou shalt not*. Wondering, I look up over my shoulder at my father.

'The swell can lift the boat sideways without warning, and swing it hard and crush your legs against the jetty and break your bones. It happened to Uncle Phil when he was boy. I've told you before, Howard – don't you remember?'

I don't remember, not exactly. I thought it was Dad whose legs were broken when they were boys. My legs are up under my chin. In place of a white bird there is only a hard object, not to be trusted.

This is my seventeenth summer. At seventeen a person is expected to be serious. Not a clown. After these holidays I will be a matriculation student, studying for my future. If I am good enough I will enter medical school.

Here in Queenscliff Dad drives our boat with great care. The tide rips through the fishermen's creek, surging and flinging our boat at its will and sudden whim, towards shifting sandbanks and unforgiving objects. As he steers, Dad's face is tense. I watch him at the wheel and

I recall those humiliating times we had to ask the fishermen to tow us off the sandbank; and that frightening time we smashed sideways against the steel uprights of the fishermen's wharf. There was a sickening crunch as the *Margot Carolin's* ribs fractured.

Through the years I watch Dad, a man struggling with the sea, doing a man's work. This is no job for clowns.

'Howard, do you want to take the wheel?'

After a day's fishing in open waters, we are entering the fishermen's creek at Queenscliff, and today, instead of driving down the creek and turning out of its riptide towards the quiet waters of the yacht club, we will tie up in the creek itself – at the fishermen's wharf.

I consider the creek. The tide is favourable: it is ebbing slowly. Its outflowing waters will oppose our progress and slow us, nature's brake for the clumsy flotsam that is a man-made craft.

Do I want to take the wheel? I know I can do it. I've done it lots of times – when Dad has been back in Melbourne. But Dad is here now. He will be watching and I will be nervous.

Again Dad invites me while the slackening tide winks at me, saying, 'Come on, Howard, take over.' Of course I do not trust the sea. She is a false friend.

I am at the wheel and the *Margot Carolin* glides sweetly down the midstream. There is a high collar of water riding at the throat of our boat, thrown up by the outgoing tide. I see it and register its silent opposition.

'Don't forget the tide, Howard. There's still a slow ebb. It will act as a brake.'

Here, in the narrow part of the creek, the air is still and we are protected from cross-breezes, but ahead of us I see ripples racing across the open water where we will make our turn before the approach. I see the ripples and take note.

'There'll be a breeze up ahead, Howard.'

Ahead of us and to starboard is the sandbank. When you hit the bank, the boat comes to a dead stop while everything and everyone aboard persists in its state of motion in obedience to Isaac Newton's Laws. A loud clatter of cups, kettles, pots, books and binoculars announces the helmsman's error, and our bruising confirms it. Then the boat leans drunkenly upon its side, a declaration of incompetence, this time quite public.

I remember that bank well, and I keep it in mind. Dad is on the foredeck preparing a mooring line. Tommy is below in the cockpit, safely out of the way of the action. Tommy is a clown. He says he doesn't know his forrard from his forehead or his aft from his arse. Lucky Tommy.

As we approach the wharf, a fisherman pulls out into the creek ahead of us. 'Go out wide to give him room, Howard, then swing in and come alongside.'

I swing the boat out wide, keeping a weather eye out to starboard for the sandbank.

'Watch the sandbank, Howard.'

I throw her out of gear to slow us for a cautious approach to the wharf, then swing the wheel to port.

'Throw her out of gear, Howard.'

As the boat loses headway a gust of crosswind blows us sideways and backwards towards the steel uprights of the wharf. I swing the wheel harder to port but the drifting boat doesn't respond to the helm. Now the tide, eddying strongly around the piles, seizes the *Margot Carolin* and pulls her hard backwards towards a large, rusty scallop boat astern of us.

It is time for some power to give us steerage way. I race the motor and slam the boat into gear.

'Throw it into gear Howard.'

The boat surges forward, away from the ugly rust bucket behind us. Meanwhile she turns hard to port in eager response to the wheel. Dad is shouting something but the motor drowns his voice. The wharf is only metres ahead of our bow and closing fast. We have no brakes. I throw the engine into reverse and rev it higher. The engine screams, the boat's forward motion slows, but too slowly. We slam hard into the steel uprights, I slow the motor and we slide penitently backwards, then I cut the motor and we stop.

Now Dad's voice is audible, clearly audible. You could hear him in Geelong. 'Howard! *What the blazes were you doing?* Why did you turn towards the wharf?'

I am quietly tying a bowline to the bollard on the wharf. I don't answer Dad because I don't have an answer.

'Why did you race the engine like that? *What made you speed up in close waters?*'

I am busily securing a stern line. 'I don't know Dad.'

'WHAT?'

'I don't know.'

I am on the wharf now, throwing an extra hitch around the bollard. Eyes stinging, I straighten and turn from the boat and walk away. There is silence for a moment and when Dad's voice reaches me again, it is gentler.

'Where are you going, Howard?'

'For a walk.'

Where am I going? It is a good question. I don't really know. I reach the end of the wharf and walk behind Cayzer's boat shed and out of sight of Tommy and Dad. There are dunes nearby and I throw myself into one of the sandy bunkers between them and settle down for a good sulk.

Afterwards, I sit and imagine the conversation between Tommy and Dad. They are sitting up on the foredeck. Dad's voice is explaining something: 'No, Tommy, I'm not angry at Howard. I am frightened for him. I want him to be safe on the water. I wanted to teach him boatmanship. Instead, I ...'

Tommy's voice would be diffident, formal, puzzled: 'Dr Goldenberg, what is there to be so frightened about?'

'Everything, Tommy. Everything is dangerous. I've lost a young man from my own boat. He drowned after a trivial mishap. I've seen the bodies of people who drowned as they fished from the rocks; I've seen legs broken – it happened to my own brother. I was sitting at his side, and a boat crushed his legs. His legs were crushed and the boat missed mine.

'I've removed dozens of fish hooks from fingers; have you ever seen that done? The hook is caught in the living flesh. You can't pull it out the way it went in. You have to push the hook deeper into the finger and force it through the skin until it comes out on the other side. Grown men sometimes faint when I do it to them …

'I've seen swimmers gashed by outboard motors, I've seen sunburn that scarred a beautiful girl's face, I've seen older people unconscious from heatstroke; and men stung by poisonous fish barbs, weeping with the pain. I've seen so much. Some people see it and don't take it to heart. These fishermen here, I've known some of them since we all were boys together. Many of them have lost family at sea. Old Alby Johnstone lost a cousin, and he himself has been wrecked twice. His boat went down off King Island and he couldn't swim, didn't have a life jacket. He hung on to floating spars until he was rescued. Then he went out to sea again, still unable to swim, still no life jacket …'

A pause. Then Dad's voice again: 'I'm not like them. I do worry. Perhaps it's through being a doctor – I've seen too much – I can't relax. I am always anxious … My father didn't know the meaning of fear. Maybe I am more like my mother, timid …'

Night is falling. They don't see me as I enter the boat from the stern, but the gentle rocking of the boat as I climb aboard will tell Dad that his son is back.

And safe.

Life of brine

The letter lies discarded. Dad's glasses lie near it and a heavy silence hangs in my parents' lounge room. Neither Mum nor Dad has noticed my entry. Dad sits with his head in his hands. At length he removes his hands and says, 'He might have drowned ...'

As I walk into the room and deliver a booming hello, the mood shifts subtly. I recognise the discarded letter. I know its contents. 'May I read it, folks?'

Silence, then Mum says faintly, 'Of course, darling.' I pick it up and read aloud:

Metung.

Dear Mum and Dad,

Real men don't eat quiche and real sailors don't wear life jackets. When this real yachtsman falls over the side of our Catalina 27 in a twenty-knot following breeze, he is not wearing a life jacket. As he falls head first from the speeding yacht, his first thought is of his own absurdity. Here he is, falling from a boat for the first time in his fifty years on boats. He is the only person aboard with any sailing experience, but suddenly, he is not aboard at all. His posture is inelegant, his body language frantic.

At the helm is Lionel. Aloft is all the sail we can carry, and we are shooting and surfing over a following sea on our way back to Metung. Lionel has never been taught how to tack, nor how to lower sail. No one on board knows how to operate the ship-to-shore radio.

As he falls through the air, our sailor grabs for the painter that tows the yacht's dinghy. But that slender rope is a slim hope and a slippery one, and it is quickly gone, leaving our sailor face downward in the sea, drinking salty water. He surfaces with another thought: grab the dinghy and climb into it; from there it's a simple matter to regain the yacht.

The thought process is swift but so is the dinghy. A frantic clutch backwards at the dinghy's gunwhale, a slither of wet hand on slippery rubber – and the little boat has made its light escape into the beautiful.

Our sailor now has ample opportunity to regard the receding yacht in its full suit of sail. How graceful, how impressive, how rapid! At the back of the yacht he can see the four lifebuoys which are supplied for such an emergency; between them are the faces of Lionel's three children as they gaze backward at him. Is that a worried look they wear? He recalls his mother's rhyme:

No matter how young a prune may be
He's always full of wrinkles.
We may get them on our face;
Prunes get 'em every place.
Nothing ever worries them,
Their life's an open book,
But no matter how young a prune may be,
He wears a worried look!

So does our sailor, because – warm weather and cloudless skies notwithstanding – he is an indifferent swimmer, these are biggish seas and no one throws him a lifebuoy. He would rather like to have one, so he raises his salt-choked voice and bellows his request. The playful wind carries his cry and drowns it in its roaring and in the humming of the stays and the crashing of the waves. The worried faces of the children are getting smaller.

One of the waves now catches him unawares and gives him another long drink. He surfaces and grabs at his hat which the sea is trying to steal from him. But he is not left naked; he still wears his green and gold Australian Olympic running shorts, an American rugby shirt in stars and stripes, and his purple running tights from the Boston Marathon. He does not customarily swim so heavily attired, but he is grateful now for all that colour; searchers will find it easy to spot him.

(Are these worried looks I see in my parents' lounge room? Can't they see the funny side? I go on reading.)

The sailor begins to swim after the yacht, but a Catalina 27 is faster than he. Suddenly the yacht changes course. In a great flapping of sails it stalls, and the sailor, greatly encouraged, swims hard for the boat which drifts and beckons only 150 metres away. He puts his head down and drives his arms and legs through the waves. After a minute of hard swimming, he looks up, measures the distance remaining, and finds it has increased to 200 metres. This is not encouraging. While Lionel tries repeatedly to drive a boat under sail directly into the breeze, the sailor swims ever harder down the wind, trying to narrow the gap, but still the gap widens as the breaking seas and the lifting breeze blow the crew further and further from their captain.

It is a tiring captain who now gives up the chase and measures instead the distance to shore. From the top of a riding wave he gazes towards Raymond Island. From this distance he can make out no detail of its tree-lined shore, no breaking wave. He knows that the trees and the waves are there to be seen, but he is too far away to discern them. Bad news.

The sailor lies now on his back, floating, resting himself while he takes a moment to deliberate. But a breaking wave ambushes him from behind, breaks over his face, fills his nostrils and ends that plan. There is no rest.

How long will it take him to swim to Raymond Island? An hour? After this morning's vigorous run on the Ninety Mile Beach, he swam in its surf, then spent four hours sailing in heavy weather. He is knackered. Can he swim for a whole hour? Can he even stay afloat for that long?

(Dad raises his head. His muttered words are a stifled scream: 'Swimming off that beach? In those rips? You had no right …' The pain in Dad's voice is sobering. My levity seems only to deepen his gravity. I read on, treading more gently …)

Until now, the sailor's breast has been filled with alarm. And salty water. Now real fear starts to take over. He knows that these waters have claimed the lives of better sailors than he. It is time not to panic; time to stop swimming and to start thinking.

I am squandering energy with all this swimming. It's not getting me anywhere. I can't get to the boat, they can't get to me, and the shore is too far away … Time to pray?

'But the sailor's tradition is to pray only with a covered head. He remembers that he is gripping his hat in his left hand. He could place it on his head and manoeuvre it into place, but that hand would be, for a time, unavailable for flotation, and a further salty drink would follow.

His ancestors wrote beautiful poetry when they were drowning. He thinks of King David's line when he was in deep trouble: From the deeps I cried out unto You, oh Lord …

Dimly he remembers Jonah. Between his time aboard the ship and his time inboard the fish, he was a man overboard like me.

In the heart of the seas,
The flood was round about me;
All Thy waves and Thy billows
Passed over me.

The sailor could do with some poetry right now – for comfort and for beauty.

(Dad snorts: 'Poetry? You need therapy!'

I can't see Dad's face. He has turned his back to me. I can see

Mum's expression, and she doesn't look her cheerful self. Why is this? Did I drown? No! Am I not here before them, hale and hearty?

I manufactured the bits about poetry. I wanted to make light of the whole episode, make it easier for them. Or was it for myself?

Writing this way, reading aloud, my words sound callous now. I stop and sit down to read on silently.)

> The sailor decides to postpone prayer; he's not desperate yet. He swims slowly towards Raymond Island, swims and drinks more brine. 'For brine is the kingdom ...'
>
> He's starting to think silly thoughts now. Not so Lionel, who has started the yacht's motor and is turning the boat about. The floating one watches with mixed pleasure and amusement the plunge and buck and swerve of a large boat under full sail, making its flapping progress upwind in his general direction.
>
> As the yacht looms close, he wonders whether the crew will recall this morning's 'Man Overboard' drill: how to slow the boat early in the approach, how to throw the engine astern so they won't run down the man overboard.
>
> In the event, neither occurs. As the boat approaches, the wind snatches the boom in a sudden jibe. The boom swings violently across the superstructure, thwacks hard against the stays, and the boat sails rapidly away to starboard, at ninety degrees from its course to the floating man.
>
> So near, but too far ... Moments later, Lionel has the boat about again. Once again she heads upwind towards its quarry, the bow rising and falling on the waves. To the swimmer, the bow looks like the head of a pony, trotting under tight rein. This time the course is unerring. Now the boat slows, now the engine whinnies as Lionel throws her astern, and the boat slides slowly alongside – but not over

– its grateful captain. Lionel's strong arm reaches down, the sailor grips it and Lionel's fingers lock around the flesh of the sailor's forearm. They look at each other. Neither will let go. The sea sucks at the sailor as he regards the ladder and the three steps he must climb to regain the boat.

A deep breath, a heave and he is free. Another breath as his tired arms lug his heavy body onto the steps. He and Lionel embrace.

Long after their short holiday, two images will stay with the sailor: both are of the skies over the lakes. The first is a picture of the brilliant blue and the blinding sun that he saw while lying on his back with the yacht receding. The second is the night sky over Picnic Arm where they rode at anchor, following the adventures of that day.

With the children asleep, the two friends took to the dinghy and glided silently over the black waters of the breathless lake. Above them was a display of the stars of heaven, brilliant and numberless. As the two gazed upward, they saw planets, the odd satellite and a shooting star. They heard the *plink, plink* of water droplets falling from the resting oars onto the lake. The brilliant stars bore mute witness as they spoke with unguarded candour of good and evil in the lives of humans; and they heard the soft plash of fishes jumping for gnats in the moonless night.

Love,

Howard

I look closely at Dad. Haggard, he looks at me, then through me, toward a distant horizon and a time long past. He sees a far place, and now – finally – I see it too. Together, we gaze in silence and see the body, limp and white, of a young man, lost on the Hay Canal.

Requiem

Dad and I have sailed hard all day. At sunset we tie the yacht to a big gum tree on the edge of Duck Arm and come ashore to eat. The ground here is littered with small sticks, fuel for our barbecue. Soon the barbecue is spitting sausage fat and sizzling lamb chops, and the spuds are charring in the ashes.

On this hillside beach there are only Dad and me and some shy cows chewing cud in the distance. Man and beast watch the night come down, and now we eat heartily and enjoy the pleasant sensations of restfulness and bodily fatigue.

Dad switches on his old portable radio, tuning it hopefully to 3AR. The reception is crystal. They are playing music on the ABC, something orchestral, something melodic and profound that I do not recognise.

Dad might know: 'What are they playing, Dad?'

'I don't know, darling.' Neither of us says anything more about the music. Before sounds like these, further speech would be rough cloth. It is dark and very still. We lie on our backs and listen to the music, looking up at a cloudless night sky. No moon, no human lights compete here with the stars.

Dad's voice crosses the nights of his four score years: 'I've never seen starlight so bright.' Nothing more is said, no rough cloth. We see light that has passed through time and space; we listen to music from another century, another continent.

We have pure light, pure sounds, deep contentment. We lie still, without speech, knowing that this is sacred, sensing that we will never again share a night like this. But neither will we lose it.

The music reaches its powerful climax, a consummation. The announcer says: 'That was *Requiem*, by Verdi.'

Joseph's three sons, 'utterly regimented'.
From left: *Myer, Phillip (Phil) and Abraham (Abe)*

Dad with his brothers and mother. **From left:** *Myer, Abe, Millie (Nanny), Joseph (Papa), Phil*

'My father the lover', at his graduation

Yvonne (my mother) aged about twenty

Myer's wedding to Yvonne, with his parents
Joseph (Papa) and Millie (Nanny)

Howard Goldenberg, aged eighteen months

Myer and Yvonne with Dennis (aged four) and Howard (aged two)

Happy times with Dad

"My father the motorist", in his Mark V Jaguar

*Leeton Infants School 1953. Third row, **far left:** Johnny Wanklyn (in jodhpurs); **far right:** Howard Goldenberg (in gumboots)*

Davening at the Kotel: Howard and Myer
praying at the Western Wall in Jerusalem, 1971

Sailing on the Gippsland Lakes. **From left:** Barry, Howard, Myer

Myer, aged eighty, honoured by 'FREE'
(Friends of Refugees of Eastern Europe)

At Myer's ninetieth birthday party. **From left:** *Dennis,*
Howard, Myer, Yvonne (front), Margot, Barry

Raphael and Emma's wedding, 25 February 2001. **From left:** *Naomi, Howard, Annette, Raphael, Emma, Rachel, Pablo*

At youngest grandson's bar mitzvah, 26 June 2005. **From left:** *Barry, Margot, Yvonne (Mum), Dennis, Howard*

Four siblings, December 2006

Four

My Father the Doctor

As a doctor, my father was widely loved and universally respected. I imagine he decided in the first place to become a doctor in order to bring honour to his parents. But in medicine, my father found work that was inherently honourable and deeply fulfilling. A doctor was a person who enjoyed both trust and authority, a person who was worthy of responsibility.

He was a rigorous medical scientist, endlessly curious about the nature of disease and its remedies, a perpetual student in post-graduate education. He attended lectures until his last months.

In the first half-century of his medical career, my father found scope in it to exercise his authoritarian nature, softening this with his gentleness and calm confidence. He was ideally suited to country general practice, where specialists were unavailable and no one encroached upon his total care of his patients.

Like farmers and many other country people, my father improvised brilliantly. At a time when heavily sedated mothers routinely gave birth to babies that were too drugged to breathe independently, my father gave the newborns mouth-to-mouth resuscitation. He took his inspiration from the story of the biblical prophet, Elisha, who breathed life into a moribund child. All this anticipated the modern practice of mouth-to-mouth by three decades. Dad never published his technique, nor felt any claim to distinction. 'I thought it was common sense,' he said.

Dad was exquisitely skilled at midwifery. Watching my first childbirth, I saw Dad coax the baby from the warm womb, caressing it into life in this world. Observing Dad's movements – precise, unhurried, graceful – was like watching ballet. As Dad arrived in the labour ward the labouring woman, gasping and thrashing in her moment of extremity, looked up and relaxed. Two lives rested securely in those gentle hands, and I wondered at my father's composure. His timing was elegant. The nursing staff respected and trusted him, and his women patients adored him. But he never fell in love with himself.

When it was over, the matron, a veteran of many births, many deaths, many doctors, walked across the room from where she too had stood watching. She came and faced me with her back to my father, then said quietly, 'If you ever become half the doctor your father is, you'll be twice as good as most.' Over the six years of medical school, I was to hear this little encomium from Matron again and again. It seemed to be a mantra, and I never tired of hearing it. I suspect that Matron and I were two of many who loved my father the doctor. In obstetrics as in much else, my inspiration came from Dad; and my love of obstetrics is inextricable from the love and admiration I felt for my father the doctor.

Happily, neither Dad nor I ever interested ourselves in what sort of vulgar fraction I became. In fact, in relation to my entire medical career, Dad was tactfully reticent, in marked contrast to his general inclination to perfect me and to control all that took place in our household. It was not until the eve of my graduation from medical school that Dad expressed his feelings about my choice of career. He said in a speech at my wedding: 'I suppose a parent might be forgiven a sense of flattery when a child chooses to pursue the same profession ...'

I suspect that at some time or other, all of Dad's children considered medicine as a career, inspired by him, even though we might have noted the drawbacks. He seldom arrived at an evening function in the same car as Mum; either evening surgery had delay-ed him, or a woman in labour threatened to call him away. My parents' marriage gave me an unhealthy example of independent spouses. Medicine gave Dad an excuse – kissed with nobility – to miss out on the lives of his grandchildren. An over-involved father became an uninvolved grandfather: austere, distant and judgmental, in painful contrast to the tender father I remember.

Some time after Dad died, Mum confided in me about an unrealised ambition of my father. The confidence took the form of a question: 'Howard, did you realise that Daddy dreamed of working side by side with you as doctors?'

'No, Mum, I didn't. I used to wonder about it. Why didn't he say something?'

'He didn't want to place you under any pressure of obligation. He wanted you to be completely free in your medical career.'

Mum had another question: 'Did you ever feel you'd like to work with Daddy?'

'I did. It was an early dream. But by the time it might have become a reality, I feared he would find me to be a clown in medicine as he had in every other practical pursuit we shared. I couldn't stand that; it would contaminate being a doctor and being Dad's son.'

And, at the very end of Dad's career, I confess that I was becoming intolerant of his old-fashioned way with patients. If we'd worked together, I might have felt critical of his authoritarian and judgmental stance. Those two elements of Dad's nature – the authoritarian instinct and the need to judge – underlay my own personal issues with Dad. I could see how they would have undermined our working relationship.

A rather sad series of events led Dad to believe that I thought poorly of his clinical work. Dad was always Mum's doctor. From Leeton days onward he was Mum's choice. In Leeton, Mum would ask him to attend to this or that medical matter, and Dad, being busy, would say, 'Yes darling. I'll attend to it after morning surgery.' Inevitably, something would come up and Mum's problem would be put off. After asking and waiting, and waiting and asking for Dad's attention, Mum would take herself into Dad's waiting room and sit down among the patients, waiting to be seen. This was highly successful.

But in their later years together, Mum suffered a series of strokes, and she saw her doctor every day and never had to wait for attention. The whole family was recruited emotionally to Mum's care. The clinicians in the family became impatient with Dad's management. The further away they lived, the less they were impressed. In particular, Dad, a product of his times, was focused on cure and untrained in rehabilitation. 'A stroke is incurable, rehab won't cure Mum.' Dad's nihilism was evident.

The family pushed for a change of GP. Mum was not keen. 'Daddy is my doctor, darling. I don't want to change.' I carried the family ammunition, Dad sustained wounds to his pride, and pain at my betrayal. In a double wound to his pride, Dad gave way to a younger doctor, a woman. (That he quickly thought very highly of her, so highly that he asked her to become his doctor as well, did not remove the cruel barb of my dissatisfaction.)

Dad spoke once of the pain – one half phrase. At the time, we were planning to go together on one of my outback locums. In heat over another issue (I recall it was the question of his fitness to drive a car) Dad said, 'I won't come with you on that locum. You'll be spared the embarrassment of an incompetent father.' Of course, Dad cooled down and did come. But his pain stays with me.

'Poor darlings,' says Mum as she hears this tale, her face a battleground of feelings. She aches for us both.

As it was, Dad and I could swap anecdotes and experiences throughout our careers. Once I became a medical student, I joined my father in a dinner-table conversation that I had first hung *upon from early days in Leeton. That conversation never stopped. Two intimate friends could share their love of the same Mistress – Medicine – until the end.*

I think my father was a doctor for too long. By the time he retired from his own practice at eighty, the world had changed. My father was masterful in the care of his patients, but once he had relinquished his own practice and he became an assistant in another, these were not the same people with whom, over decades, he had danced that intense dance of life and of death. These were new people, often with new ideas.

Dad was taught to be master of the clinical scene, but contemporary patients were consumerist, seeking not a master but an equal. Yet they were not Dad's equals in clinical understanding, and he often found their demands trivial and tiresome. They were no longer the people whom he had brought into the world, whom he had counselled and succoured, whose hands he had held through grief and pain. They were not the people who had moulded him; he was not 'my doctor' to them, just another old medical geezer.

Why then, did he continue to practise for so long? Clearly, the fear of financial want in retirement was a motivator, but I suspect that Dad – gardener, seaman, carpenter, welder, French polisher, shipwright, cook and mohel *– had lost those extracurricular pleasures to rust and to Time. A shy man whose brothers and cousins and friends were taken from him, one by one, by his Grim Colleague, Dad found society only at work and at* shule.

So there he was, creaking into his nineties, still working for fear of stopping. And when Dad did stop doctoring, it was because he could no longer drive a car. So he took up a new cause: the care of my mother, with her manifold disabilities. Now Dad could still serve. He could direct Mum's doctor in her doctoring, and direct Mum's carer in her caring. And he could serve the woman he had always loved, free now of competition from his Mistress.

At the schoolyard

There is a man sitting in a car outside the school. He just sits in his large black car, sits and waits. We can see him from the classroom. The man in the car looks back in the direction of the school, his gaze fixed. There is nothing to see at the school except for the buildings. They are not so interesting. But the man sits and stares, sits and gazes, his mind moving upon the silence.

Then the bell rings. Straight away children pour into the yard from all the classrooms – every class except ours. Instantly the children are all playing games. The girls are skipping, the boys are playing footy or chasing tennis balls. There is a game of chasey and another of hidey. Between and among the running games, girls play hopscotch to its measured and stuttering rhythm. The air fills with cries and laughter. Weaving throngs form and dissolve; the yard is alive.

Our class is not allowed out for morning play. We are having detention. Mrs Savage is punishing us for something: for not sitting straight, or for speaking in class, or for breathing too loudly. Detention is an opportunity to sit straight and not to speak and not to breathe. There is nothing to do other than to sit and look at the man who sits and looks at the school.

The man in the black car is very interested in the children of Leeton Infants' School at play. He winds his window down, he leans forward, looks hard, listens hard. He looks like he could eat the children.

The bell rings again. This is the signal for the playing to stop, but the games continue. A teacher strides into the playground, blows a whistle, and the throngs of children unravel and file into class. The watcher in the car watches the last stragglers as they melt away and only the buildings remain, staring blankly back at him. He sits for a moment longer, then abruptly starts his car and drives away. He has spoken to no one, approached no one. Now as he drives away I can see a smile flash across his face.

I know that car. I recognise the man. He is the local doctor. He is also my father.

At lunchtime, Mrs Savage releases us and I walk home for lunch. As I come through the front door, I hear Mum and Dad talking. There is something about their voices that holds me. I stand and listen. Dad and Mum are saying things in grown-up words. They look serious.

I ask them what is wrong. Mum looks at Dad. Dad looks at me. Then he sits down. 'I have a patient who is very sick,' he says, 'and I am worried about her.'

'But Dad, you can make her better ...'

'No, darling. She has a sickness that I can't cure. No one knows how to cure it. It's called cancer.'

'What will happen to her, Dad?'

Dad is quiet. He doesn't want to answer me. At last he says, 'I am afraid she will get very, very sick. I will have to give her very strong medicines to stop her pain ...

'You know, Howard, I felt very sad after I saw that sick lady to-day.' Dad stops again and looks at me for quite a while, gazing just like he did down at the schoolyard. Then he says, 'When I was sad this morning, Howard, I went to the school. I came and I watched the children play ... that's what I do when my work makes me sad.

'When I was a student at the university in Melbourne, I would often see people with terrible sicknesses. Afterwards I used to ride my bike to the big library in the city before I went home, and I would sit down and read fairy stories. The happy endings made me feel better.

'And that's what I was doing this morning. I watched the children playing at the school. Children are a sort of happy beginning. After a while those happy beginnings made me feel better and I went back to work.'

The doctor

I drive along Wellington Parade in East Melbourne, heading for Carlton and the coffee precinct. It is spring. I have a belly full of warm food and a yen for coffee. The sun shines through my car windows and all is very well with the world as my car seems to drive itself towards Carlton.

But the road ahead is blocked by a group of people, apparently squatting in a circle. A bicycle lies on the ground in their midst. The body of a cyclist lies next to it. The rear wheel of the bike turns slowly on its axle, but the man is quite still. These people might have been painted onto the roadscape.

I pull over and get out to investigate this still life. I approach the circle. The figures are women, all looking with concern and indecision towards the cyclist. Slowly they come into motion. Very slowly, the man sits up, cradling his left forearm in his right hand. He says, 'Get me a mobile phone …' A female form rises from the tableau. She flits swiftly away and returns, bearing a phone.

The cyclist is a fair young man, lean, lightly muscled, probably good looking. But at this moment his face is very pale and pearls of sweat bead his forehead. He is injured: two bones, long and ugly, protrude through the soft tissues of his forearm, their ends jagged. The white bones, bloodless, naked, torn from their covering of flesh, are an affront, a violent challenge to the way things should be. I stare at those bones – there is the radius, there's the ulna – but their Latin names do not domesticate them or make them less shocking. All is not well with the world; I am shocked and an ancient fear grips me. I know I need to do something helpful, now!

I address the man: 'I am afraid your arm is broken.'

'I know that.' His reply is measured, assured.

I try again: 'Let me help you off the road onto the plantation. You don't want to get hit by a car.'

His right hand grips his shattered left forearm. He says, 'I can walk there myself.'

'Let me help you – I'm a doctor.'

'I can manage – I'm a doctor too.'

He crosses from the roadway to the plantation, wobbling slightly, then sits abruptly on the grass. He indicates the phone and says, 'You can dial triple zero and call an ambulance if you want to help.'

I call an ambulance. Then I retrieve his bike and put it into my car, and insert my card into his pocket so he can claim his bike when he's ready.

The injured man tells me that he is a surgeon. He has given some thought to his choice of orthopaedic colleague. He gives me a telephone number. 'I want to speak to him myself,' he says.

I dial, holding the phone close to the cyclist's ear. He speaks: 'Murray, it's James. I need you to reduce a couple of compound fractures for me … this afternoon … radius and ulna. They're a bit of a mess. They'll need some nails and a plate … No I can't do it myself … *because I'm the patient – that's why!* I'm waiting for the ambulance. I'll see you soon.'

He rings off. Paler now, he lies down on the grass, and closes his eyes and waits. I stand to one side, nonplussed. Then a similar scene, from another time, comes to me.

❋

It is a Sunday afternoon in Leeton and I am alone in the house, reading. Dad is working in the shed and the others are out. There are sounds coming through the back door – a banging, a slamming, a thump, then silence. I look up from my book and listen. Now the sounds come again. My book is forgotten and I am on my feet, ready to flee from these heavy footsteps that thump towards me, now closing on me. But it's Dad, running towards me, running with his head bent forward, one hand gripping the other.

'Bring the phone – quick!' Dad's voice is urgent, half a shout, half a grunt. The voice has an edge that I don't recognise. It frightens me. I return with the phone and offer it to Dad, but he is still gripping his wrist tightly. The muscles of his face are tight too; he is frowning and clenching his teeth. He looks angry.

'Put the phone on the floor,' says Dad.

I do so. Then I see the blood. It trails from the hall back through the kitchen and leads to the back door.

Abruptly, Dad sinks to his haunches, pale, looking inward, marshalling his strength. The great red blotches on the floor, the white of Dad's face, sap me. I stand, helpless. Dad grunts something: 'Howard – you can help me. Get me … a clean tea-towel from the kitchen … and a wooden spoon.'

I hear that unfamiliar something in Dad's speech. It frightens me more than the blood. And why is he asking for kitchen utensils? It doesn't make sense, but that edge of urgent command speaks clearly enough. I run, ransack kitchen drawers and return with the objects. Dad releases the wrist from his grasp and grabs the tea-towel. Rapidly he opens it then folds it lengthways into the shape of a stout bandage.

Blood, bright red, spurts in an arc from somewhere on Dad's hand. Surprised, I stand still, detached and fascinated. The fine stream squirts upwards from Dad's hand to the level of his heart, then outwards in a slow arc and splashes against my breast. Now my eyes turn to the source of the stream, a linear gash down his left wrist and the heel of his hand.

The flesh is laid open. The inside of Dad's hand is a valley; its white walls glisten moistly. On the valley floor a little red spring launches the blood. The white astonishes me. I look and I cannot move.

Dad's hand is cut open and his blood is everywhere. I don't know how he can bear the pain. I feel fear to the bone.

As suddenly as it started, the bleeding stops, then starts again, then stops. *'Damn … and blast … I've hit the artery!'* Dad is angry again, speaking in grunts and gasps as he inhales, wrestles with the bandage, holds his breath too long, then sucks in the next lungful of air, struggling all the while to apply pressure to the pulsating artery.

Dad wraps the bandage around his hand, keeping pressure on the palm. Then he grabs the wooden spoon and, in the moment of release, the white tea-towel reddens. Dad pokes the handle of the spoon between his skin and the bandage, then twists hard. With every turn of the spoon, the bandage tightens. The hand goes plum-coloured, then white, and the bleeding stops.

Now Dad speaks more normally. 'Darling, hold the phone near my ear.' I do so. Dad speaks again: 'Operator, please get me Leeton 29. Thank you … Hello, Weekes? It's Myer. I'm glad you're home. I'm sorry to disturb your Sabbath, but there's an operation that I need you to do today … I can't do the surgery myself – *I've done something stupid … gashed my hand with a chisel* … (that angry voice again) … It's pretty deep. There's an arterial bleeder … I've stopped the bleeding with a tourniquet. I don't know if there's any tendon damage … if there is, we might never operate together again.'

Dad falls silent, listens intently, nods, then says, 'Thank you, Weekes. I'll be here, ready, as soon as you arrive. …'

Now Dad asks the operator to connect him to the hospital. I hold the phone while he speaks to the head nurse and books the operation that his friend, Dr White, will perform on him. He turns to me: 'Put the telephone down, Howard.'

I notice that Dad says *telephone* differently from other people. He says *tellyphone*.

'Thank you, Howard. Come and sit down here next to me.' He pulls me close against him. Dad's good arm is around me and the world is well again. Suddenly Dad lets out a deep sigh and lies down flat on the wooden floor. His face is wet and very white. Beneath the twisted tea-towel his injured hand is white. He doesn't move until Dr White arrives and takes him away in his car.

I sit and wait for Mum and the others to come home, then I tell them that Dad cut his hand and Dr White is making it better.

A few days after my aborted trip to Carlton, a letter arrives.

Dear Howard,

Thank you for caring for my bike. My arm is nailed, plated, plastered and in a sling. I won't be doing any surgery for at least three months. I hope I will be able to go back to operating in due course.

The night before my accident, I was sitting down to dinner with my partner. We were asking ourselves the question: How can I find a way of slowing down?

Thanks again,
James

I show Dad the letter from James, then recount my memories of the chisel episode. Dad gives me his smile that says: 'Howard, you have an overactive imagination.' He can't see the connection.

The needle

Dad is in his seventies but his spine is about a hundred. Over many years, Dad has treated his back without mercy and now it takes revenge. That back has humped heavy wooden boxes of olives on the farm, hauled boats up and down beaches, hefted dinghies onto heaving decks and bent over numberless operating tables over more than fifty years. And now Dad is paying the price.

Dad's back has been hurting badly for a month or so. Yesterday it became suddenly much worse. Dad seeks the advice of a doctor who knows the patient well, the only doctor whom he trusts to do his bidding. That doctor is Dad himself. He refers himself for an x-ray, then reads it himself, pointing out to the redundant radiologist the numerous abnormalities he sees.

The spinal joints have been obliterated by deposits of calcium: tough, mean little spicules of bone, each one of them a spot repair of some injury done by passing time and by Dad himself. Where once there were moving parts, there is now a rigid scaffold pitted with crags that pinch and stretch the spinal nerves.

Back home, in pain, Dad views his films with grim satisfaction. 'Look at that, Howard,' he says through clenched teeth. He demonstrates the chunks of calcium that are blocking his spinal canal. 'That's spinal stenosis; it's squeezing the cord. And look at that ...' (he indicates the place between two vertebrae where there should be a strong disc to protect the nerve) '... that space has gone. I've prolapsed that disc. I did it lifting some flagstones yesterday.'

Dad isn't speaking normally. He grunts his words in painful syllables. He continues: 'I'm numb in my leg, here, and in awful pain up here.' He points to his thigh and buttock. Then he says, 'Give me some pethidine, please darling.'

I look at him in surprise. Dad is tough. He seldom acknowledges pain. Even when stricken with his annual blinding migraine, he won't concede that it is actually painful. It is only 'real discomfort', bad enough to take a single painkiller. Dad knows from old experience what true pain is – that's the screaming pain of renal colic. After his one experience of the kidney stone (forty years ago) Dad will never drive into the country without taking a syringe and an ampoule of pethidine.

Dad holds in affectionate contempt those who whinge with pain that is less severe than renal colic. This includes his children and most of soft humanity. When we have pain, we complain of it early and loudly. And Dad has a horror of the easy slide into narcotic addiction that so many doctors create for their patients.

Now he is writhing before me and requesting pethidine, a narcotic. He looks at me with simple trust. But I don't see this simply at all. While I stand and consider, Dad is becoming desperate. His voice has never sounded like this before. He is begging, begging *me* – *his son*: 'Please Howard. Hurry. This is unbearable.'

It is unbearable for me too. I run to my doctor's bag and draw up the injection. I administer it without giving a moment's thought to the religious law that forbids a child to hurt a parent, to draw even a drop of blood, to create – God forbid – even a bruise. If I had in fact considered the law, I'd have ignored it happily. The pain of the needle, the blood, the bruise all seem positively sacred. What is profane is the suffering that renders my father helpless, a supplicant upon the mercy of his own son.

The injection gives Dad some relief. He dozes. This gives me leisure to consider again what I must do. A single injection won't cure Dad's problem. He will need treatment for some time. Who will be his doctor? So far, Dad has been perfectly content with his own medical care, but he needs help now. He obviously anticipates that I will do the job. I know that I cannot, and will not. I rehearse my arguments. 'Dad,' I'll say, 'I want you to get another doctor. I don't want to give you injections of pethidine. I won't be happy doing it against my judgment, and I won't be happy to withhold it if you are asking for it. And what's more, I think you should be in hospital. You need care around the clock and I couldn't do that even if I wanted to.' This seems to me a pretty convincing argument. It convinces me.

I wait for Dad to stir. When he does so, it is pain that awakens him, intense, mounting pain, an inrushing flood tide that knocks him sideways.

'Dad, you need to go to hospital ...'

'I need an injection.'

'Dad, I can't treat you like this.'

'Why not? It's simple – just relieve the pain. Just do it. Don't talk about it.'

'Dad, it's the wrong place, I'm the wrong doctor, you're the wrong patient, it's the wrong treatment'.

'What are you talking about, Howard?' He looks up from the floorboards that he favours as his sickbed. He searches my face for signs of stupidity; then for compliance; finally for compassion. He does not find his answer. Now he is begging me – again!

'Dad, listen to me, please.' He winces and looks at me again. Impatience gives way to anger, then to a broken spirit. Dad has been moaning. Now he is screaming. I try once more: 'Dad, this is what I will do. I'll give you the shot but only if you'll agree to go to hospital.'

Dad looks at me with disbelief, then with black resentment. He bends his head. 'Give me the shot,' he says, 'and do what you like.'

But there is nothing I can do that I will like.

I give him the injection, then make a final effort to be fair and dispassionate. I call his friend, Jeffrey, an older doctor than I, to come and help. Dad respects Jeff, and Jeff loves and honours Dad as if he were his own father. But that, as it transpires, is the problem. Jeff does not want to rule this indomitable man. He agrees that Dad should go to hospital.

I call an ambulance and they take him away – fearful, resentful, mutinous. I want to wish him well, to repair the damage. 'God bless, Dad. Get better.' He does not look at me.

Thirty-six hours later Dad is out of hospital. He hasn't worked for two whole days. He goes straight back to the clinic. This repairs his deepest injury. Rapidly I am his son again, not his doctor; and he is my father, not my patient. Dad is sovereign, beholden neither to man nor drugs. Where the nerve supply was cut, the muscles of his right leg are wasting and he has a patch of skin which will never have feeling again.

He forgives easily, but he does not understand. 'How could you withhold the pethidine from me as you did, Howard? How could you deny any patient that relief from suffering?'

I try to explain, but Dad cannot fathom my inhumanity. Grudgingly he comes to respect my stubbornness. That is a familial trait. Finally he concludes that I must have been suffering from blindness. He does not blame me, but he cannot understand my motivation at the time when my father lay before me and screamed for my mercy.

Perhaps I was blind. Perhaps blindness was necessary.

In the time that follows, we seldom advert to the matter. When-ever we do, Dad speaks without heat, but with wonder. To the end of his days, Dad shakes his head and does not understand.

Once more unto the breech

I have a friend who is expecting her first baby in a few weeks. When her delivery date comes, I will be in a far place, doing an extremely remote locum. So we meet now for a talk.

Kristie is excited and nervous. 'The baby's a breech,' she says. 'I can't have a natural delivery in case the head gets stuck. The doctor's going to do a Caesarean section.'

My mind goes back to the breech babies I used to deliver. In those days, GPs delivered babies, both head first and bottom first. Those were the days when a vagina was a vagina was a birth canal, and a caesarean section was a relative rarity. Older now and wiser to the risks of breech deliveries, I am glad that Kristie's doctor is protecting her baby.

As Kristie and I sit and talk, I recall a recent dream. 'A few nights ago, I dreamed I was delivering a baby. Would you like to hear my dream?' Kristie would.

'Labour ward phoned me to tell me that a patient of mine had been admitted in labour and would soon be ready for delivery. In the dream I knew that this patient's baby was a breech presentation. But the mother had previously given birth to big babies, so I wasn't too worried that the head might get stuck. I had time to get out my father's volume of *Practical Obstetrics*, a textbook by Professor Bruce Mayes. This was the book Dad used to refer to when preparing for any complicated delivery. During Dad's heyday as a country GP, Prof. Mayes was the doyen of obstetrics at Sydney University. Dad valued the book and admired the Prof. as warmly as I admired Dad for his obstetric skill.

'Now, with Dad no longer alive, I went to his old bookshelves to find *Practical Obstetrics*. There it was, just where I remembered. There were the diagrams that choreographed the whole complicated ballet of breech delivery in a series of graceful steps.

'And I went to Labour Ward and I delivered the baby, and it was healthy and the mother was happy and I was skilful and graceful.

'And then I woke up. And I was smiling with the pleasure of it all.'

Suddenly I realise that I am about to cry. Kristie looks at me and I do cry. I cry for the sweetness of bringing a child into the world, and I cry for the memory of the man who showed that sweetness to me.

Five

The Man at the Wheel

To my young eyes, my father seemed a master of all practical tasks. He was certainly a confident and safe driver. He enjoyed motor cars that were well engineered, and his tastes were conservative and British.

Everyone in our district recognised Dad and his vehicle; I felt proud of my father the motorist. As I saw it, Dad ranged across our country district far and wide in his car, bringing care and cure wherever he went. I imagined that everyone saw Dad's car as an extension of this good man in his service of the community.

Always a rather timorous small boy, I was sometimes appalled by my father's fearlessness and calm in the face of danger or emergency. It seemed to me that there were perils besetting us on all sides during our long trips, and Dad seemed too much like Sir Henry Newbolt's Captain Drake: 'Roving, though his death fell, He went wi' heart at ease ...'

In my childhood, my seatbelt was Dad's strong restraining arm; and in my adolescence I discovered that this man at the wheel understood deeply how hard it was for me to become a man.

My father drove cars from his childhood into his dotage, driven at first by a sense of adventure and at the last by a sense of duty. In the course of nearly three score years in cars together, I saw my father's progress from mastery of his fate – when he was a king on the road – through struggle, to a sort of acceptance of the tyranny of Time.

That my father could not submit without this struggle was a small tragedy and quite characteristic. That I felt compelled to intervene was also characteristic of the son of that father. And my intervention brought us both pain.

My father the motorist

Some of our greatest adventures come to pass with Dad at the wheel of a motor car. In the early 1950s Dad drives a Mark V Jaguar. It is big and black and fast. In this car, Dad opens up the atlas of the great world. He is the navigator and the driver, the master. The land lies before him, and at his command the miles fall away and our riverine flatlands give way to hills, seas, lakes and new rivers. Dad compasses a world larger than the wide imagination of a child.

Our car is the only Jaguar on the roads of the Murrumbidgee Irrigation Area; no other car can catch us. So Dad sometimes has races with Constable Bulley on his motor bike. The constable waits for us in hiding among the willows on the Yanco Road. When he sights us speeding towards the river, his motorbike erupts in a roar of sound and there he is, all silver and black, chasing our car of black and silver. After Dad and he have had a race, Dad stops and has a talk with him, and the policeman writes things down in his little book.

The river itself is mighty. Huge gum trees line its banks and the water is swift, deep and cold. Where the water sweeps around a bend there is a beach of coarse sand. We build sand castles on the beach. Other children build castles which rhyme with hassles – ours are not the same: ours rhyme with parcels. We say it differently because Mum and Dad are originally from Melbourne, where people speak English.

You can drown in the river. I am watching from the bank on the day that Dennis nearly drowns. It is exciting. Dennis steps from the beach into the shallows, then turns to Mum pointing to something he has seen. As he turns, he stumbles. The fast water knocks him over and takes him out into the stream. Dennis doesn't say anything so I don't either. Mum looks up and doesn't see him. Dad is higher up on the bank, telling Nanny to try one of the egg and tomato sandwiches. Mum asks where Dennis is, and Dad doesn't know. Then I tell her and she is on her feet, running. She runs to the river, yelling. She starts to go into the river but she remembers she is carrying something in her arms – it is the new baby, Margot. She stops at ankle depth, one arm holding the baby, the other extended towards the fast river and the boy disappearing fast around a bend.

Suddenly Dad is there, running down the bank, then airborne in his plunge, then swimming and grabbing Dennis by his ginger hair and then they are both back with us on the bank.

Mum and Dad have a conversation about whose fault it is. Dennis wanders off and takes a couple of the egg and tomato sandwiches.

The whole thing is memorable: it is the first time and the last time that I ever see Mummy run.

Back in the Jag, Dad drives more slowly than usual. Dennis is sitting in the front between him and Mummy, and Dad's hand is on his knee. When he asks Dad to open the roof he does so, and when he stands up with his head through the roof, Dad allows it. With all Dennis' ginger hair on show, old Constable Bulley won't be able to miss us on the Yanco Road.

My friend Johnny Wanklyn says, 'Your Dad and his black Jag are famous. Everyone around here reckons your Dad is crawling at thirty; he's warming up at eighty, and he's only hurrying when he gets to a hundred miles an hour.' I feel proud to hear this.

One day the big fast car helps Dad to save a patient from going blind. He is a farmer whose eye has been slashed open by the wild end of his fencing wire. He needs an urgent operation in Sydney, and his plane to Sydney will leave Wagga in ninety minutes. The ambulance is not available. The distance is seventy miles and the Jag can do it easily. Dad and the farmer set off, and soon he has the Jag warming up nicely to eighty miles per hour.

Dad comes to a bend in the road and applies the brakes. Nothing happens. Dad tries the brakes again – nothing. Inside the big car, three eyes widen as they approach the small bend at speed. 'Hold tight!' A slow experimental pull on the handbrake and a desperate changing down of gears – somehow the car is around the bend and the road stretches straight ahead.

Dad decides that the injured Jag can now only safely crawl. And crawl they do to Wagga's approaches. As they reach a crest Dad recognises, at the distant foot of the long slope ahead, the bridge that will take them across the Murrumbidgee and into the city. The bridge is a long one and it runs at an angle to the highway. They will have to deviate far to the right of the road merely to enter upon the bridge. The car picks up speed as it descends the hill. Dad is calculating angles, speeds and roadholding.

Now the bridge is upon them and they enter from the right lane, trying to tame a runaway from the wrong side of the road. Providence takes the wheel and they are through – just before the school bus enters from the Wagga end.

A pause at the first milk bar in Wagga for an urgent phone call to the airport, then Dad is skirting Wagga by back roads, hastening with frantic slowness, and sliding into the airport, onto the runway, into the path of the DC3 which is waiting for them. The Jaguar makes a timely stop and Dad hands over his patient.

After repairs, Dad brings the Jaguar home. He sits down to eat lunch with us and tells Mum the story. Then he goes back to work.

Dad and his car traverse the known world, taking four small children along unsuspected byways to unexpected waterways and to new places and pleasures. When Sunday dawns he packs us into the Jag and the roads lead us to Young, where an orchardist urges us to pick all the cherries we can eat.

Another time Dad says, 'We're going to the Hawkesbury.' I anticipate a place of hawks and berries but the Hawkesbury turns out to be another river. This one, however, has salty water! We unpack the Jag and live on a boat for seven days. Dad drives the boat through calms and storms, beneath crags and into bays. We sleep on the boat and shower under a waterfall.

Dad drives us to Orange, another misnomer – where one again expectation fails to bear fruit. Instead we watch Dad fight for our lives; we are speeding around a bend on a dusty road behind Orange when we hear a sudden explosion. Then the Jaguar goes berserk: it throws itself towards the road's gravel verge and Dad wrestles it back onto the narrow road. The Jag then careers off in the opposite direction and again Dad strains to tame it as it rises and leans on its side, first on two wheels, then on the other two. Backward and forward the demented giant plunges, and a terrible roaring and shuddering is felt from below and behind as we go.

Finally we come to rest. Dad sits quite still. Mum turns to Dad, wondering. We see her in profile. Under its canopy of lovely black curls, Mummy's face is very pale. At length Dad answers her wordless question: 'Blow-out!'

Dad and Mum get out and Dad shows Mum the ribbons of rubber that were once the nearside back tyre. Mum puts her hand to her mouth, then opens the back door and holds each of us close for a moment as we emerge. Then we all watch Dad as he jacks up the car and changes the wheel.

In autumn Dad drives us along roads that never end through the Snowy Mountains to Talbingo. The road is a corkscrew and, as I peer from the window, I can see no footing for the wheels – only precipice and certain death below. Urgently, I call out a warning about the road that isn't there, but Dad drives calmly on. The abyss does not frighten him.

We reach Talbingo. Here is a river so shallow and so clear we can see its bottom, a bed of smooth stones. Fishes swim and beckon through the crystal waters. We enter the knee-deep river and we discover a coldness so sharp it thrills. We children of the dusty plains are used to turbid rivers that roil and eddy. We have never imagined places and rivers like these that our father finds for us.

We never return to Talbingo, but its cold clear waters run through memory undimmed. You cannot visit Talbingo today; it has been drowned for electricity by the Snowy River scheme. It lives now only in the verse of Kenneth Slessor and in the bones of those who trod its bed. It was Dad who took us there in time to see '… waters huge and clear / Lopping down mountains / Turning crags to banks'.

Floods come, and at Yanco the Murrumbidgee breaks its banks, creating an inland sea which stretches far away below a curtain of grey mist, beyond the limits of seeing. We are in the car, cut off by the floods from our home. The rain is falling and the waters are rising, and I can picture them drowning a black car and the family within. The night falls darkly around us. We leave the road and drive across soaked pasture for higher ground. Then the worst happens: we get bogged.

Dad opens the car door. He is about to go outside. I am stricken with fears too terrible to voice: will Dad be lost in the unseen floods? Will we be lost? Leaving us to contemplate our fate in our silent ark, Dad plunges into the wet and dark. Before long he returns with a lantern, accompanied by a farmer who tows us with his tractor, bringing us safely to the other side.

When summer blazes and the bitumen roads of the Riverina melt in the sun, Dad drives us one hundred miles to the tiny town of The Rock where, with astonished delight, I enjoy my maiden ice cream – the only kosher ice cream this side of Melbourne; or to Tocumwal where the waters of the Murray cool our blood; or to Jerilderie, where Dad enters a pub! – a place of swelling sound and sinister glooms

– emerging with a whole bottle of cold lemonade. There is frost on its glass. One swallow does a summer unmake.

Sometimes Uncle Abe shares the driving with Dad. As we drive, they recall their first driving days together. Dad describes how he, Uncle Abe and Uncle Phil used to take their father's car 'for a spin'. They were only little boys and they didn't have the keys. Two would push and the third would steer. Once, the brothers pushed Dad so well that the car tipped over when he went around a bend. They had to face their father after he found his car, lying on its side a block from home. I think about their father (my Papa), a man of heat and fearful thunder. Somehow Dad and my uncles all survived.

On one occasion Uncle Abe and Dad are driving us from Leeton to Melbourne when they decide on a short cut, a detour through the back streets of Coburg and Brunswick and Carlton, the haunts of their childhood.

We swing left, away from Sydney Road. 'Here's the school, Abe ... there's the bookshop ... look Howard, that's the house where Uncle Abe and I lived when we were your age!' (Were they really once my age, children, small boys?)

'Here's the bakery, Myer. Let's stop for a minute.'

They return to the car, both talking volubly – the shop is just the same, the baker has aged, he's an old man, how old would he be? Dad carries a bag of bread-rolls and another, smaller package which seems more promising. Inside that bag are flat biscuits studded with sultanas and poppy seeds, and coated in the reddest jam I have seen. These are the exotic foods of a great city. Dad and Uncle Abe have tracked them down in Dad's car.

There are bandits that hold up motorists on remote roads and rob them. I have heard Dad and Mum speak of them. Once, we travel a dirt road that never ends and takes us through far places where there are few houses and fewer faces. In the distance we see a shape in black and white on the road ahead of us. We slow and make out a man with a black hat and a white shirt; the collar of the man's shirt is back to front. He stands next to his suitcase. Dad stops the car and asks him where he is headed. 'No,' says Dad, 'we aren't going that far.'

Good, I think, let's close that window and get going. But no, Dad is speaking to the man, offering him a ride, apologising. 'We can only take you the first hundred miles, then we turn off and have to leave you …'

The man gets into the front. He carries his jacket across his arm. What does that jacket conceal? I keep my eye on the jacket for the entire one hundred miles. We arrive safely at the turnoff and the man gets out. Luckily for us, we had nothing he wanted to steal.

When a car stops suddenly, a child can be thrown forward against the windscreen. If thrown through the windscreen onto the road, the child can die. Dad has had to treat small children who have been hurt in this way. But Dad knows how to keep a child safe. He applies the brake and, as the car stops, my small frame becomes airborne. Then he extends a strong arm to his left. My ribs collide with Dad's arresting forearm and I bounce off him and back into my seat. In this manner I travel safely by land and by air over the ways of boyhood.

The last of these journeys from my rural home takes place when I am nine. Dad drives me to the city and I never again live in Leeton. Unknowing, I have been driven across a line in time. From now on I am a city dweller.

There are other journeys. The journey of greatest discovery takes place during one of our occasional weekend drives from Melbourne back to Leeton. Dad and Papa are going to count their losses on the olive farm at Stony Point. I come along for the journey, and to visit Johnny Wanklyn. I am now about fifteen. Sitting in the back, I am half-listening when Papa complains about Tom Saunderson's discourteous conduct towards him. 'He saw me, he knows me, but he didn't speak to me. He just stood there – *shtumm!*'

Dad's response staggers me. 'Father,' he says, 'don't you realise that Tom is shy? Don't you understand that he sees himself as a simple farmer? He's self-conscious enough merely trying to make conversation with the doctor, but with the venerable father of the doctor, he's completely overawed.'

Then Dad says something unimagined: 'You know, Father, a person can feel so shy and confused and lost for words at times that he wishes the earth would open up and swallow him … Howard knows how that feels.'

A flood bursts inside me. Yes! Yes, that is how I feel. How could Dad know what I never said, what I tried never to show, what I scarcely knew myself?

That flood feels very warm. I am not alone, never again alone with that feeling. Dad understands how I feel. This tide of feeling, of relief, of love between us has reached its high water mark within me, and it persists and never ebbs.

Now that I am a teenager, I become a desperado of the roads. Like Dad, I like to borrow a car – Mum's – and take it for very short, very fast drives up and down the nearby dead-end streets. I find you can get to quite a decent speed on some of those lanes and streets before you have to jam on the brakes and stop. I never tip the car over and I never, ever take Dad's car for a spin. I lack the death wish.

Dad's father is getting old. He still drives his big old Chevrolet. He drives down to Queenscliff for a bit of fishing and when he returns a week or so later, the Chev's rear bumper is missing. It turns out that Papa was travelling along the Geelong to Queenscliff road at precisely the same time as the weekly train was crossing. He never saw the train. The train did not stop and Papa scarcely noticed as something clipped his tail, amputating the bumper.

Dad and Uncle Abe and Uncle Phil pay a visit to their father and confiscate his keys. Soon after, he sells the pale blue Chevrolet and he never drives again.

When I turn seventeen Dad teaches me to drive, and now we are both motorists. These days Dad drives a Humber. It is humbler than the Jag but it has plenty of power. We take an overnight drive from Melbourne to Leeton. Halfway there, Dad decides to take a nap. 'Take the wheel for a little while, Howard. Don't go too fast.'

I take the wheel and I don't go too fast – until Dad is fast asleep. That Humber can go a lot quicker than Dad drives it. I get it up to eighty miles an hour and he sleeps on. I get it up to ninety, then inch up towards ninety-five … I am nearing a hundred when the shape on the road ahead comes suddenly very close and without warning moves across our path. I slow, swerve left, narrowly missing the milkman and his horse and cart, and apply the brakes. Dad stirs. He glances across at the speedo. It reads 80 mph.

'Slow down, Howard!'

'OK Dad.'

When Dad turns eighty we throw a big party. Dad is still a busy doctor, still driving.

One day, as he drives away from St Vincent's Hospital after operating, something clips his tail but he does not notice. Later he receives a summons for failing to stop after an accident. A barrister convinces the court of Dad's palpable innocence and he continues driving.

Margot and John visit from America and he drives them and Mum down to the yacht club where he keeps the boat. The gear lever inexplicably selects *Reverse* instead of *Drive*, and the car races backwards in the direction of the water. Somehow it stops just before the water's edge. Dad can't imagine how the car came to malfunction like that.

And Dad keeps on driving.

Through Dad's late eighties and into the nineties, trees, parked cars and signposts make scrapes and dents on his smart red duco. He becomes a frequent customer of the panel beaters. He laughs off suggestions from his children that he should stop driving.

Finally, his three sons confront him with their concerns: no, we are not taking away the keys – who would dare to? – who would wish to? We have come to inform Dad that I (the only one of four children to follow him in a medical career) have decided to notify the licensing authorities of our misgivings about his driving safety.

I tell Dad that he is the best 91-year-old driver I know; but he isn't as good as he was when he was eighty-one. He is good-natured and patient as he explains away my misconceptions. Equally courteously I tell him that I am not convinced. I will notify the authorities. Let them determine whether his hearing, his reflexes, his coordination, his eyesight, mobility and concentration are up to the mark.

Dad is grievously upset.

Once, years ago, Dad and I were travelling from Leeton to Melbourne and listening to *Julius Caesar* on the car radio. When the great man becomes at length blind to his own hubris, his followers join together to kill him. Caesar recognises his friend Brutus among his assassins. Together Dad and I share the shock and the pain of betrayal as Dad translates for me Caesar's last words: *Et tu, Brute?* – even you, Brutus? Now that the day has come for me to assassinate my father the motorist, I recall those words. Does Dad recall them too?

The licensing authorities tell me they are very cautious about acting on reports of 'unsafe' drivers. They get lots of malicious reports. But if the report comes from the driver's doctor they give it greater weight. So I couch my report clearly: 'I am not the driver's doctor. I am his son. Further, I do not state that Dad is unsafe – only that I think he needs to be assessed.'

The response of the authorities is swift and unexpectedly high-handed. They suspend Dad's licence immediately and invite him to undergo testing.

Equally swiftly, Dad accepts the invitation. Then he settles down with an ally who will coach him for the written test of the road laws. The coach is one of his sons, one of the gang of three who came to him in the comfortable arrogance of middle age to take away his independence.

My brother Barry telephones me later to tell me of his plan to coach Dad. 'You'll probably kill me for helping Dad, Howard, but I reckon he should be helped. I can help him with the rules, but I can't make him into a safe driver. If he isn't safe, he will fail the practical test, but if Dad passes, I reckon he's earned the right to keep on driving …'

I don't feel like killing Barry. I feel like kissing him.

Meanwhile Dad tells everyone he knows, 'Howard has taken away my licence.' And he informs me that he will not accept any offer of a ride from me. Dad is still independent.

Only now can I start to make sense of Dylan Thomas' lines addressed to his father:

> And you, my father, there on that sad height,
> Curse, bless, me now with your fierce tears, I pray.

Dad sits the written test of road rules and passes with flying colours. Then the occupational therapist takes him for the road test. Afterwards, he tells me with great satisfaction that she is very impressed with his driving. One thing only prevents her passing Dad there and then; when changing lanes, he doesn't look over his shoulder to check following traffic. (Who does? I certainly don't.)

The occupational therapist books a further test. Meanwhile Dad is still off the road, still declining my offers of transport, still telling the world of my perfidy.

Now he has his eyesight test. The result is borderline. He takes his specs to the eye doctor who tweaks the prescription, then he undergoes a further eye test. And passes it. Dad takes his second road test. He looks over his shoulder at every opportunity and the tester comments favourably on the change.

Then he waits.

The letter comes while Dad and I are away on holiday, together with Dad's beloved cousin Bob. Bob is a doctor in America where he is a genius in the narrow corridors of the Ears, Nose and Throat. (The 'Goldenberg Ear' is his invention. I don't know whom we can blame for the Goldenberg Nose.)

During this holiday Dad, Bob and I work together in a number of outback Aboriginal communities. It is the belated realisation of an old dream of ours. Later, Dad tells everybody (as usual), 'it was the best holiday of my life.'

On his return to Melbourne Dad collects his mail. Bob is with him as Dad recognises the stationery of the licensing authority. Bob watches him tear it open and read the news: the licence has been renewed. He sees Dad vindicated, triumphant – but as he leaves the next morning for the States, Bob is troubled. Dad calls me, trumpeting his news over the phone. He is exultant. He has won. My own feelings are mixed.

That morning Dad drives to see his doctor. After seeing her, he pulls out from her parking bay and drives directly into the path of a following vehicle. Did Dad look over his shoulder? I do not ask. Dad says later, 'That driver must have been driving very fast.' I feel dismayed.

In the collision, the driver's child bumps her chest. Dad checks her out and tells the mother her little girl is all right. They check the child at the hospital; she is all right. And Dad is all right.

Dad gives up driving at night. This decision means he has to give up his work as a doctor because he can no longer drive home from the practice at night. After sixty-eight years in work that has brought him honours, it must be a hard decision.

At ninety-one years of age, Dad no longer goes to work. But he has a job to do, and no, he cannot delegate it. It is his job to look after Mum, and that requires him to drive a car.

No, a taxi won't be adequate. Dad is adamant. Is it a matter of independence? Or simple thrift?

I want Dad to stop driving. 'Dad, you'll save money if you sell your car and take cabs. It will be safer. You won't have to park. Somebody else can worry about looking over their shoulder ...'

Dad is smiling. It is an affectionate smile. It says: Howard, you mean well, but you don't understand. I need to drive. I have to look after Mum.

Now I get it. It is a matter of honour.

One last try: 'Dad, let someone else help.'

The smile is there again, a barrier against mild persuasion. It says: Howard, save your breath. We can talk like this all day and still be friends. You can talk and I'll keep smiling. But if you want us to remain friends, don't try to force my hand again.

Then he makes one concession: 'From now on, I'll only drive to the bank and to see the doctor ...' I recall the previous occasions when I have seen Dad rage, rage against the dying of the light. I do want to remain friends. I keep my peace.

But a year later, when Dad is ninety-two, and battling so hard to stand against a sea of troubles that he can no longer see the shore, Dad's sons act. One son takes to driving him to every known appointment. Another tries to anticipate his shopping and banking needs and runs errands.

But Dad drives on and into things and too close to things.

I prepare another letter for the licensing people, another doctor's report that is not a Doctor's Report. This time I do not propose to confess my action to my father. But before I post my letter, someone else (who? – who cares so much that they protect him from himself?) tips off the authorities that Dad is categorically unfit to drive. Dad asks me whether I am playing Brutus again.

'Not this time, Dad.'

He accepts my word. The authorities send him a letter requiring him to visit his eye doctor for a further examination. Dad drives to this appointment. It is a longer drive, more complicated than the short trip to the local doctor. There are confusing junctions to negotiate, awkward parking areas, unfamiliar school crossings.

Now Dennis, the firstborn son, takes decisive action. He confiscates Dad's car keys as well as the spare set, and announces to Dad what he has done, and why. Dad raises no protest.

The next day Dad drives to his usual haunts. He has a third set of keys, carefully hidden against just such a time.

That son visits the police station nearest Dad's home and announces in advance the larceny which he is about to commit: 'My father is old and frail and unwell. I believe he cannot drive safely. I am taking his car away from him. If you receive a report that his car is missing, believed stolen, here is where you can find me.'

The firstborn hands the police a slip of paper with names, addresses, registration number and phone numbers. Then he visits Dad and says, 'Dad, I am taking the car away from you.' Dad raises no protest. He does not inform the police of his son's Illegal Use and Possession of a Motor Vehicle.

To me, he does confide that – prior to my brother's action and irrespective of it – he had already decided not to pursue his driver's license. 'It is my independent decision,' he says.

A document arrives at Dad's address. It is headed:
Notice of Suspension of Driver Licence No. 3151172.
The letter advises the addressee that, according to their records, the licence holder has not undergone the driving test prescribed in their recent letter. It further advises that, pursuant to Regulation 303(1)(a), the licence will be suspended, effective 14 November 2003, in accordance with the authority delegated to the writer by the Roads Corporation.

The letter is dated 31 October 2003.

But the letter has no effect. It has been preceded by another, dated

24 September 2003. That letter is in the form of a certificate that records the death of Myer Goldenberg, aged ninety-two years, on 10 September 2003.

> Old age should burn and rave at close of day;
> Rage, rage against the dying of the light.

Verses quoted from 'Do Not Go Gentle into That Good Night' in The Poems of Dylan Thomas; *and from Kenneth Slessor's 'Talbingo' in* Six Voices.

Six

A Philosophy of Walking

My father did not fear death. But he did fear disability. And he had a special horror of cancer and stroke.

He knew no other way to live, even in great old age, than by ignoring his own aging. My father was uncompromising in respect of his age: he gave no quarter. He had succeeded in his life by the exercise of an indomitable will. As he saw it, even in his giddy nineties, willpower would see him across the road safely, unaided. One night I found him on the footpath, bloodied in a fall onto a major roadway. He had gone out for pizza because Mum had a whim for it. He had not thought to phone for delivery, he would not call upon one of us to help. And here he was, in the hands of the ambulance officers who were cleaning and binding his wounds. I caught him correcting and instructing them in their bandaging technique.

Dad rejoiced in his independence. He was not about to allow anyone to help him; rather he should help others.

And Dad knew his duty: he was Mum's husband and her care was his job, his prerogative. Anyone who presumed to help was a usurper.

There was a snatch of a ballad that Dad liked to quote from his boyhood:

For Witherington needs must I wail
As one in doleful dumps;
For when his legs were smitten off,
He fought upon his stumps.

After Dad retired from medical practice, the task of caring for Mum was his sole reason for being. It literally kept him alive – fighting upon his stumps – until it quite literally killed him.

Dad lived for so long, gritting his teeth against pain, that by the end he seemed scarcely able to know pleasure. Barring those few sweet moments when he held one or another of his new great-grandchildren in his arms, Dad's last months were measured only by the degree of his pain and by the incursions of disability. As his flesh weakened, Dad tasted humiliation for the first time since his childhood.

In this inescapable grief of life, even Dad's final outback holiday brought him no joy. A friend helped me to take him on a trip through the Flinders Ranges. We had tailored it for his delight, calculating carefully his capacities and matching them with his interests. Dad loved all science including geology, mining, biology, meteorology, astronomy. Here was a visit to Wilpena Pound, there an off-road drive to old mines; a joy flight over salt lakes and rugged crags and verdant oases; a night session viewing the desert stars from an observatory. Through all of this, Dad could only chafe. In this late chapter of his life, a holiday was as great a trial as his life at home. These days, I seldom saw him smile.

And in all our time together I never saw him weep. He did not surrender, he never enjoyed the relief of tears, of sharing grief in our arms.

Dad's devotion to Mum was inspiring. I felt it was noble. It made me weep to see it. At the end, however, where we children looked for flexibility in our father we found him rigid. We fought with him. The conflict between our father and the children he had moulded *was probably unavoidable. But for me at least, it was intolerably painful; after a lifetime of amity and harmony together, I saw us moving towards an end, tense and frustrated with each other.*

Before we needed to, each of us was losing a friend. Is this – perhaps – how we prepare ourselves for an end, that we contrive these means of creating small distances, fissures that will widen into the final rupture?

But there were moments of mildness, of quiet acceptance and real intimacy …

Walking

A restless man, my father believed in walking as other people believe in an abstract ideal. He believed in its implicit values of exertion and of independence. I think its austerity appealed to his thrifty soul. He walked as he lived, impatiently and energetically. He made little concession for the lesser powers of his small children.

Dad seemed to appreciate the Socratic value of conversation afoot. Moments of discovery, of the dawning or deepening of understanding attended our walks together. I learned from Dad's example the meaning of stamina. I learned about courage and about its limitations.

In Dad's later years, I witnessed his inconsistent and ambivalent responses to his aging; his early philosophic acceptance of aging and of dying, and later, his contrasting practical refusal to 'go gentle into that good night'.

During these walks I was confronted by intimations of my father's mortality. Dad and I worked daily with mortality. Our conversations were full of it and I felt that I was philosophically prepared for the phenomenon of death – that of my parents or my own; but during these walks and talks Dad seemed to see Death beckoning to him and I realised how unready I was for the loss.

Walking with my father

It is late on a *Shabbat* afternoon in the cabin at Tidal River. You have read all the papers, Dad, you've had a nap and you are full of restless energy. I am full of the opposite.

'Howard, let's go for a walk.'

A walk in the late afternoon in summer promises mosquitoes, sand flies and sweat. I am pondering the rival attractions of my book, more food, more sloth.

'How about a game of Scrabble instead, Dad?' – a compromise.

'No, come for a walk with me,' you say.

'OK, Dad.'

We set out for South Norman Beach, walking along the track between the ti-trees, climbing steadily. As we climb the steep inclines you are breathing comfortably. At the top of a rise, you suddenly break into a run, and within moments I am alone – fifty metres behind you.

Immediately, this walk is like all the walks we have taken together over more than forty years; you are well ahead, I am well behind, and we are both more or less at a loss. After all, you did say, 'Come for a walk with me.'

Do you remember walking together to the hospital in Leeton, many years ago? It is *Shabbat*, when you will not drive except to save life. You are checking on some patients whose surgery you performed yesterday. I am five years old and you are forty. You step out, striding ahead, and I have no difficulty in keeping pace with you – so long as I run almost all the way.

A few years later, *Shabbat* finds us walking together again, this time in Melbourne. We are walking to *shule*, making haste for the start of the service. As my running gets stronger, I keep pace with you more easily over the six kilometres that you walk each way to and from Toorak Road Synagogue.

Neither of us anticipates that I will run marathons in middle age, but it is these walks with you that condition me physically and mentally for distance running. By the time I reach seven years of age, you have taught me the spiritual basics of completing the marathon: *if it matters enough, I can keep on going.*

A pattern emerges in our walks together. Your striding legs and my scurrying feet pound out this pattern and consolidate it until it becomes a Law. As you would have it, the Law reads, 'I am walking alongside Howard, my always tardy son, so I must be running late. I had better go even faster'. My reading runs, 'If I'm walking with Dad – who has to arrive early – there's no hurry'. A corollary of my Law is that we might as well slow down.

So it is that two people who adore each other and truly relish each other's company set out together for numberless walks over very many years, but seldom arrive simultaneously. Both you and I carve in stone our law, with our strong legs, our strong will and our stiff necks.

You, the Patriarch, know that it is not for you to accommodate a tardy son, while I, the son (a deferential mule), come to sense that I might never catch up; and perhaps I should not try to bridge that distance which has become destiny. Perhaps this constant distance is metaphor for one who follows faithfully in a father's footsteps – or one who is uncertain how to do so.

Bemused, I watch your downhill gallop over ruts and between rocks that bestrew this steep path. What possesses an eighty-year-old to dart off in this manner? And how ungainly is that gait that threatens ever to tip you into the tea-trees and to fracture one of your silly old bones, 'O bone of my bone and flesh of my flesh ...'

That familiar gait – who else runs in that awkwardly efficient manner? The answer is a revelation: it is I, your son, who runs after you. You are waiting for me at the bottom of the hill with an explanation.

'I like to break up my walks with a run every so often. The different rhythms prevent my joints stiffening as they age.'

That's right Dad – I've seen your brain darting and racing to keep your mind from stiffening. Yeats knows how you tick:

> An aged man is a paltry thing,
> A tattered coat upon a stick, unless
> Soul clap its hands and sing, and louder sing
> For every tatter in its mortal dress.

We have reached the beach now and have begun our return to the river. Here there are no hills and we keep pace with each other comfortably. The day is coming to its mild end. We are walking together and talking of all manner of things.

'A small whale beached itself here and died last year, Dad. I had never seen one so close. It was a small whale, maybe fifteen metres long. Even dead it was majestic. I felt very small.'

'Howard, they were flying kites on the beach here this morning, great big box kites. I've always loved kites. I've never seen a kite fly so high.'

We stop for a moment or two and gaze around. Behind us in the sand stretch two long lines of footprints, now parallel, now separating. The footprints start at the south end of the beach and follow us all the way here, ending at our feet at this turnoff alongside the river. Our walk is nearing its end. We face inland and walk now in the shade of the rocks and the ridge. You point out to me the shapes of cloud and rock and bank that you know well and love from previous visits. Your voice is firm and clear and poised.

But it is the voice of valediction I hear. I turn away a little. Oh Dad, Dad, 'Do not go gentle into that good night / But rage, rage against the dying of the light ...'

It was many years ago that you advised me to read Hemingway's *The Old Man and the Sea*. I did read it, being then about the age of the boy Manolo, who loves the old man, Santiago. As the book closes, Manolo weeps for the old man who lies asleep before him, exhausted. But Santiago knows no sorrow. He is dreaming of the lions of his youth.

And the two walked together

Today my father does not die but he comes close. He is a stubborn man and I am an optimist. In the wilderness, stubbornness and optimism can be a dangerous combination.

I have been working at the clinic at Jabiru in the beautiful Kakadu National Park, and today is my day off. Dad and I get up at dawn and empty our bladders. On any ordinary day this physiological function would not be worthy of remark. But this will be a long day of dry heat.

We say our prayers, eat plenty and drink little, then drive to the mountains. A winding dirt road brings us to a camping ground at the foot of steep hills. Here, in glorious heat, we admire a little waterfall that tumbles two hundred metres to a pristine pool.

There is a notice by the pool that reads: NO FISHING. THE FISH IN THESE WATERS ARE PROTECTED. Some fat barramundi swim complacently at our feet. These fish don't look frightened. We reason that there are no crocodiles here. We have a dim recollection that crocs like estuaries but not waterfalls. Reassured, I jump in and cool off.

I emerge and we eat huge chunks of watermelon, then look around and consider what we'll do next. Dad looks up at the waterfall. Filaments of water wind and wander downwards with slow curves and sudden plunges. The slim ribbons of water widen as they pass over a broad shelf of rock then leap in a shatter of lace and mist, down to trouble the surface of the tranquil pool.

The fall of water draws the eye down, down, down to its consummation at the pool; then the eye, still hungry, butterflies up again to the lip of the escarpment to '... where the pine-clad ridges raise /

125

Their torn and rugged battlements on high ...' I feel the pull of the slopes, their green and their shade; I feel the allure of water and life in a place of heat and stones.

But it all looks pretty rugged, too rugged for a man in his eighties. I float an idea: 'Dad, how would you feel if I zip up to the top for a bit, then come down and join you for a picnic?'

Dad looks at me as if I am stupid. 'Let's go,' he says.

Dad's heart is an old model, now discontinued. Over the years, most of that batch have been recalled by the Maker; but Dad's heart ticks on, somewhat erratically nowadays – especially on uphill gradients. He has some medication for emergencies, which he has prudently brought with him to the Territory. Later, I will discover that Dad carefully left the medication behind in the car before our hike up the escarpment.

Dad and I skirt the pool and find a track that leads up to the cliffs. The track is steep, its surfaces uneven as it winds between rocks and trees. Even where the shade dapples the track, the heat is fierce; and wherever we emerge into the open it is brutally hot.

Dad climbs adroitly, his old feet seeking out stable surfaces, testing them for give and for slip before trusting them with the weight of his frame. I watch Dad in the hard going. He is a quadruped, climbing with arms as well as legs, reaching for the next sapling, pushing off from the last. The arms, once powerful, are thin now. The skin hangs loosely from the muscles where the subcutaneous fat used to be. I watch those gnarled hands and wasted arms as they use the slender trees as a balustrade.

Dad is dogged. He brushes away my helping hand as he grunts and strains on the steep bends. It is a brave effort. At every stop, I offer Dad a drink of water. At every stop he declines my offer.

From time to time he stops for breath and trades pleasantries with the young hikers who puff and pant past us. Some of them are coming down, wearing only bathers. They have wet hair and they look cool. They tell of a series of rock pools, a couple of metres deep, formed by the creek at the summit, just before it becomes a waterfall.

When we make the summit Dad is a little shaky, so I sit him down to rest. I am feeling concerned and I beg him: 'Dad, please drink some water.' Dad looks at the bottle of water then gives me a look. I know what he is thinking: That's just water in that bottle. You know I never drink water. The bottle lies at my father's feet.

I turn and follow the ridge line towards the promised cool of the pools ahead. The track winds its narrow way between shrubs and low trees, then ends in a wide clearing. Here, perched midway between earth and heaven and fed by the stream, are three pools of cold clean water. Young people are getting into and out of their clothes. Some are sunbathing on great granite boulders, while others frolic in the water. I enter and cool my blood while listening idly to accents from Scandinavia and Japan, Ireland and Germany.

I clamber from the first pool to the second, then to the outermost of the three, where I gaze out far beyond the falls to the green of the distant forest on the valley floor. Here in this pool you can – if you choose – sit on the very lip and look down to the distant barramundi pool below, down, down to the void, down to extinction.

A few of the visitors from far countries are doing just this. Blithely, they chat and frolic and splash each other, one or two of them astride the rock, another with his back to the falls. Fascinated, paralysed by vicarious fear, I sit and think horrific thoughts.

Time passes. Suddenly I remember Dad. I leap from the pool and race back to the track where I find him simmering nicely in the noonday sun. His water bottle is hot to the touch. And full. 'No,' he says, 'I haven't drunk; I'm not thirsty.'

He stretches out a hand: 'Help me up, Howard.'

Dad's skin is very hot and not sweaty at all – the skin of a person who has run out of body water, one too dry to sweat. He is unsteady on his feet. He looks like I feel at the end of a marathon, but he still has half his race to run.

We start our descent. Dad lets me support him now. It is slow going. Dad is breathing rapidly, laboriously. After a few minutes we stop for a breather. When he's ready we resume, more slowly now. Dad is heavy on my shoulder and it is hard to take his weight and to keep him stable on the rough track.

A phrase comes to me from a Bible story as we descend. It is from the story of another father and his walk to a hilltop with his son: the father is Abraham and the son is Isaac. It was Dad who first told me this story, the account of a father who loved his God enough to kill his son; and of a son who loved his father enough to allow him to do so.

The phrase that recurs during our downhill struggle is ... *and the two walked together*. Generally, Scripture is very economical with words, reiterating only where necessary for emphasis or nuance. In the Abraham story, the phrase *and the two walked together* appears twice. The repetition expresses an abnormal closeness between father and son: father and son walk the same path.

Dad and I walk and walk, two bodies stumbling, entwined, now on four legs, now three, sometimes two. Time is forgotten as we wrestle and stagger. Time and again the phrase plays in my head.

Our rests are becoming longer and more frequent. I beg Dad to drink. Finally he opens his mouth and moistens his tongue, a token drink to please me, no more. This time he takes his rest break seated in a scrap of shade. While Dad rests I think clinical thoughts, thoughts of fluid loss and dehydration, of heat stroke and failing kidneys. I calculate the travel time to the nearest medical help, at Jabiru. At Jabiru there will be little equipment and only two doctors – both GPs – one of them his son.

After twenty minutes or so, Dad tries to rise but he cannot. I help him to his feet but his legs buckle. I sway beneath his weight, my tears moistening his dried-out pate. Dad's weight is heavy and it is light. I clutch him, hold him close, reluctant to sit him down again. Any passer-by who witnessed this improbable gavotte might wonder why a middle-aged man and his aged father chose this spot and these means of expressing their love.

'Let me down, Howard.'

I do so, heavy with guilt. I am composing phone calls to my brothers in Melbourne and my sister in New York. In my mind I refer solely to clinical details, to emergency retrieval by the Flying Doctor, to the Intensive Care Unit in the hospital in Darwin, to a great heart that has failed at last. I steer these mental conversations away from my complicity in Dad's collapse.

I do not compose any excuses for Mum. She never blames any of us for anything.

Dad lies on the ground. I crouch over him and watch. He is still and he makes no sound. I look around us. Over my left shoulder, only seventy metres away as the crow flies, is the car park. A man with a fair beard is seated at a picnic table, reading. I am on my feet, running, not following the serpentine track but the crow, plunging straight down the slope to the car park, to the picnicker who sits and reads innocently below.

Fairbeard looks up at me in surprise, listens for a moment, then rises and races with me up to the old man whom we find lying, inert, in the shade by the track. We take a shoulder each, throwing Dad's arms about our own. Four legs hurry along and around and down the track, while two others swing above it. We make our vehicle, a four-wheel drive belonging to my employers. Carefully, gently, we lay Dad down and buckle him in.

A wave, a word of thanks, and we are on our way, driving fast. The 4WD has fiercely efficient aircon, and all vents are blasting cold onto my Dad. He lies there and does not move and does not speak.

We come to the ford across the first creek. I jump out and race to the water's edge to fill my hat with cool water. By the bank there, I see a notice that says something about crocodiles, but there is no time to read it. Back in the car, I upend the hat over Dad's face. Now he has both speech and motion. He gasps, half sits and says mildly, 'Thanks, darling.' Then he lies down and falls asleep.

It is 200 kilometres from the waterfall to Jabiru. About two-thirds of the way there, Cooinda comes into view, the site of a wonderful cultural museum that exhibits the features of the land, its flora and fauna, and the life of its people.

Dad says, 'Let's stop and have a look, Howard.'

Over the next hour the old fraud walks around the exhibits, reading, studying, absorbing everything. He leaves reluctantly. He says, 'Thank you darling. That was very moving.'

Back at Jabiru, I drink with a mighty thirst while Dad sips abstemiously. It is the next morning before the camel, my father, empties his bladder.

Lines quoted from 'The Man from Snowy River' by A.B.Paterson

Fighting on his stumps

The first morning in Port Douglas is hot. The old man, nearly ninety now, walks jerkily, dodging the lances of pain that shoot up his wasted legs towards his twisted spine. His son has gone for a long run and the old man is alone in the apartment.

The old man wants to walk to the beach, half a kilometre away. All his life he has loved the sea, and this will surely be his last seaside holiday.

> I shall wear white flannel trousers, and walk upon the
>   beach,
> I have heard the mermaids singing, each to each.
> I do not think they will sing to me.

With painful slowness, the old man walks down to the beach and sits for a while on a fallen tree trunk, bathing his stained, veined old legs in the outgoing tide.

Then he winces his way back to the apartment, where he sits down and grins to himself.

The next day is hot and sunny. The old man feels the pull of the tide and once again he walks down to the sea. He is gone a long time and his son begins to wonder, then to worry.

When the old man returns, his grin is too big to hide. He asks his son, 'How far along is the nude beach?'

'Six kilometres.'

The old man sits and calculates, reckoning the gap between potency and desire.

Every day the old man goes out walking and returns, smiling – each day a little later.

The seventh day is the last of the vacation. The sea is a sapphire. The old man sits on the edge of his bed, looking down at his legs. The sea, the sea, he feels its pull. Up now and walking, up and hurting, hurrying his steps, taking shorter steps to spare his hips, his back, his knees, his sacroiliacs. Running now, now walking and feeling no pain, the old man is a young man; he is flowing along the beach, flowing along the river of his years, flowing six kilometres to the mermaids who lie at the furthermost end of his days.

> We have lingered in the chambers of the sea
> By sea-girls wreathed with seaweed red and brown
> Till human voices wake us, and we drown.

The old man is walking to his long home.

Verses quoted from 'The Love Song of J. Alfred Prufrock' by T.S. Eliot

Whale Mourning at Wamoom

'Wamoom' is the Aboriginal name for Wilson's Promontory. Dad loved Wilson's Promontory. He claimed, somewhat unconvincingly, that he did not love poetry. He would sooner be dead than read a poem.

Naturally, I dedicate this poem to him.

My father walked these hills and steeps;
Woke early ever, walked rugged rock-strewn track
To the lookout, and back. Now he sleeps
Forever; and I rise with the sun
On this second day of the last new moon
Of the dying year,
And sound the *shofar*, the ram's horn warning,
Then go for a run on a crystal morning.
My father walked till his dying year; I follow his track
Across the bridge,
Then up the hill and over a ridge –
Then back; pausing to view a sapphire sea.
High here, on air, at Wamoom, this southern
End of a continent,
Comes remembrance, a fifth element.
Midst earth and water I stand, content,
Basking in the gentle fire of an early sun,
Then turn
To start the slog and gasp and sweat – up hills
And tracks on the ridge of the returning run.
'Stop!' – cries the voice of my companion –
'And turn!
And look out to sea, and see – there's a whale!'
I stop and turn and look – and sight the sail-
Shaped fin, the hump of back, the mammalian
Brown-black, a bruise
On the blue face of the sea. Now it sinks again
And as I smile, give thanks and muse
It surfaces and plays, and sprays its spume
At the end of the dying year.
Another whale was here, beached, dead; while with my
father
A decade ago, I saw it. We paid homage at its sandy
tomb.

Seven

My Father the Lover

A Persian carpet

No sullen tropic sun shall wither
The roses in the rose-garden which is ours and ours
    only
But this dedication is for others to read:
These are private words addressed to you in public.

(T. S. Eliot in 'A Dedication to my Wife')

The charismatic young rabbi of the Melbourne Hebrew Congregation introduces one of his young lady congregants to another of his congregants, a young medical graduate. History records that this rabbi will rise to the greatness of Chief Rabbi of the British Empire, but it is this one small act that combusts and creates a family and its history.

My mother reports on the man she meets: 'a most decorative young man'. She speaks of him as one might of some aesthetic phenomenon – cautiously protecting herself with humorous detachment.

And so my parents meet, fall in love, marry and have children. Paradoxically, these essentially private acts will create the loss of privacy: their children will become witnesses to their parents' lives.

I am a witness. This book bears witness to the lives and the love of my parents. In the course of a lifetime as witness, I see some things that make me proud, some that make me glad, others that trouble me, confuse or distress me. Lives that for so long ran parallel, intersecting infrequently, became, at the close, asymptotes. In the graph of my parents' intimacy, two separate lines grew to be even closer.

A sensitive child, I often misgive.

When I am older and my own marriage is no longer new, I sense the durability of my parents' love. It is like a Persian carpet that the weavers lay out upon the cobblestones for the traffic to toughen; we children pass boisterously through our parents' lives, and leave them much as they began, a man and a woman alone together. It is their business how they love each other.

It is none of my business.

It is all of my business.

In setting out to write a memoir to pay honour to my father, I resolve to write only such things as will bring him honour. Initially I decide to act the severe censor whenever I feel a tension between loyalty and fidelity. Then I realise that a book of partial truths would be a hollow compliment to a man whose life turns upon fidelity to the truth. I come to understand that there is nothing I know of my father that is disgraceful – even his warts have their nobility.

Can I write truly of the father I love? Have I the right to speak of my father the lover? The question might be posed differently: have I the right to exclude these stories of my father the lover? So I do write of these things.

In these matters, I take Dad's feelings as my guide. During Dad's later years, when what I write is unflatteringly critical of him, I read the piece to him. He laughs the laugh he reserves for all of my writings, and bids me not to worry. Dad simply appreciates my serious attention to his life. He never doubts my love.

In this book, I write my secrets. But what of secrets that do not belong to me, secrets sacred to the couple who create and nurture me? Those that are known to me are few. Those few sparkle with the dew of love. But they are not mine, so I ask my mother to censor this section. As a watchdog, Mum would lick an intruder to death. This least censorious of parents smiles. She cannot see the point, but she humours me.

She reads the drafts and weeps and keeps them by her bed. They bring back to her the man she loved.

'Can I publish these, Mum?'

'You can publish anything you write about Daddy, darling.'

I see things that are crystals of delight. One evening, Dad and Mum emerge from their bedroom wearing special clothes. Dad is wearing a dinner suit and Mum is wearing a ball gown. 'We are going to a ball,' they say.

'What is a ball?' we ask.

'It's a party with dancing,' they reply.

'What sort of dancing?' we wonder.

Then Mum and Dad break into a crazy sort of jig. The gaiety of it, the syncopated movements, the crazy jumping, waving, laughing spirit of it amazes us. These are our parents, grown-ups, leaping for the love and joy of it, leaping like lambs in the spring. They stop dancing and catch their breath.

'That was the Charleston,' they say.

I see things that are the stuff of tragedy. In caring for my mother, my father retires from the heroics of a medical life and emerges upon an intimate stage where he plays out the final act. He lives and dies on that stage, Mum's heroic lover.

My father the lover

It is *Seder* night, the first night of Passover. We sit around the table
– my mother, my father, my older brother and I, all sitting at Nanny
and Papa's great big table of polished wood, all sitting and trying not
to get growled at by Papa. It's not easy.

The table is crowded. Over there on the far shore are my cousins
Ruthie and Carmel, and my Uncle Abe and Auntie Claire. South and
west of me sit cousins Berenice and David, with Auntie Becky and
Uncle Phil. And at one end sits Nanny, small and wrinkled, while
Papa, round and fierce, is enthroned at the other end on his couch of
leather, a free man reclining and celebrating the Festival of Freedom,
presiding over the tribe he created in this country.

Beneath me, this chair has legs of polished wood, legs that are
longer than mine. My legs swing and occasionally drum against the
polished wood. The drumming brings Papa back from ancient Egypt
to the noisy present, where a noisy grandchild, lacking in polish, is
removing the polish from the tribal furnishings. Papa remonstrates,
his wrinkles swelling in his quick fury. His whiskers bristle with men-
ace. If Papa had said to Pharaoh, *Let my people go*, we'd have been out
of Egypt like a shot. But here in East St Kilda, I shrink into my chair
and I miss my home in Leeton.

Behind Papa is a tiger. He has an arrow protruding from his back,
which he arches in fury at the unaccountable pain near his spine.
Where the arrow has entered, the tiger's coat of cream is stained with
blood. The tiger is of marble. He looks cross. He looks like Papa talking to his tribe. I sit quietly and keep an eye on that tiger. I try not
to breathe too much.

Resting before us on the table of polished wood are brightly col-
oured books, *Haggadahs*, books which tell the story of how we were
saved from slavery in Egypt. I sit quietly, trying not to breathe.

I open my book and read: In every generation, a man must see
himself as if he went out of Egypt … And you shall tell your son on

that day, it is on account of what God did for me, when I went out from Egypt ...

My father has the most beautiful of all the *Haggadah* books. Its cover of dark navy blue, alternating with a royal blue, is framed in gilt. Its colours are gorgeous, like gold and lapis lazuli plucked from some Pharaoh's tomb. Did Dad bring it with him when he left Egypt?

Dad is leaning to his left, a free man, leaning and singing at his ease the songs he knows by heart, songs of his exodus from Egypt – where he was a slave. While he sings, I open Dad's *Haggadah* at the wrong end, the way you'd open a book in English. The *Haggadah* falls open and from it falls the likeness of a princess. She has short wavy hair and dark eyes. She smiles at me and at the young man who took her photo. Smiling like that, she might conquer a young man's heart. Those eyes are fanned by lashes longer than the whip of a taskmaster. There's a mole on her round cheek that sends a message, urgent and imperative – come close. I begin to sense what enslavement might be.

Dad has stopped singing. His gaze has fallen upon the picture and he is smiling a sudden and bashful smile. His face is red. 'I knew her once ... a long time ago, when I was in England ... Her father wanted me to marry her and live there in England. He offered to buy a medical practice for me if I would settle down there with his daughter ... but I wanted to come home, here, to my parents and to my brothers.'

Dad is speaking to me but all around the table the singing has stopped and people are listening. They crane to look at the picture, then they turn quickly and look at Mum, checking her reaction. She smiles benignly, a queen secure on her throne.

On the wall behind Papa is another photograph. Like the one on the table, it is black and white and it too is a life-size shot of a face. Full cheeks, dark hair, broad shoulders and a shy smile – and around the shoulders you can see the academic gown of a young man on the day of his graduation from medical school. He is smiling across the room, surveying the world he is about to conquer. He looks like the sort of man a princess might want, the sort of man that a merchant in Manchester might choose for his daughter. I begin to see my father differently.

I recall the phone call that I answered the other day, back in Leeton. 'Dad is out,' I tell the lady, and I pass the phone to Mum. She nods as she listens. 'Yes,' she says, 'I understand how you feel … Yes, yes, he is, isn't he? … Yes, I agree. Yes, very … very handsome indeed.'

Mum smiles at me across the room, smiles and nods her head at intervals, murmuring assent. Her smile widens and she says, 'Yes, he is very kind … No, no,' – now her smile is huge towards me – 'no, of course not, no, not at all … Yes, I'll tell him you rang. Bye-bye.'

'That lady thinks Daddy is wonderful,' she says. 'And kind. And clever. And patient. And so very good looking. But,' adds Mum, 'the lady says I mustn't think she is in love with Doctor.'

Mum pauses and smiles again. 'Of course she's in love with him … I know how she feels; I love Daddy myself.'

Aunty Claire is leaning across the *Seder* table, leaning in Dad's direction, giving him a look. 'Myer,' she says, 'tell us about that other girl, the one in Euroa.' Dad is blushing again, mouth opening upon words he'd rather not speak. He shakes his head but Claire is not giving up. 'Tell us, Myer. We all want to hear.'

Dad looks around, but no one comes to his rescue. He looks a long question at Mummy. Her smile and her shake of the head tell Dad he need not say; she knows him, she trusts him. Dad starts to relax, then his gaze falls once again on the Princess of Manchester, and when he looks up and speaks, it is to us boys.

'I worked as a locum once for a doctor in Euroa. It was a long time ago, long before I met Mummy.

'The doctor went away and I lived in his house while I filled his place in the practice. He was away but his wife stayed in the house.

She was friendly and kind to me – I did not know anybody in the town – and I was glad when she invited me to go with her on a picnic by the river on my afternoon off. It was sunny down by the river, and we ate and I fished, and she told me about her life. I felt quite flattered by her attention. She was older than I. She was … quite attractive.

'She said she was lonely. She was not happy in her life with her husband; and in that moment I realised she wanted me to fill her husband's place – in her life. That was a wrong thing she wanted me to do – to steal a man's wife from him. He had gone away and he trusted me. He left his patients and his home and his wife with me; I wouldn't do something like that.'

Uncle Phil mutters an aside: 'Potiphar's wife …'

Dad continues, 'As soon as the doctor came back, I left and I didn't explain.' Dad is quiet now. The whole *Seder* table is quiet. The tribe breathes out. Papa is looking at his son and he doesn't look fierce. He clears his throat and we go back to our *Haggadahs*, back to the telling of the story of how we got out of Egypt.

Falling gums

The phone rings at midnight. I walk towards the answering machine and listen for an urgent message. I do not pick up the receiver because it is Friday night, my Sabbath – *Shabbat* – when my soul visits paradise. When I am in paradise I do not answer the phone. There is no message.

Though puzzled – who would want to speak to me at midnight if it were not an emergency? – I begin to relax, then the phone rings again. Once again my machine offers to take a message, once again the caller is mute. I grab the phone. Dad's voice says, 'Mum is on the floor …'

'I'll come now,' I say, and hang up. Dad and I have responded to the situation with the least possible desecration of the Sabbath.

Minutes later I let myself into my parents' house. There, on the bedroom floor, in a tangle of limbs, is my mother. 'Hello darling,' she says. She looks up at me and gives me a grin. Recently, Mum's front teeth have begun to desert her. Those teeth that remain are a picket fence, stained and in disrepair. Mum's former serene smile has given way to a seven-year-old's grin – all mischief and careless abandon.

I peer down at Mum's legs. They are thin, too thin, except for her ruined knee which is swollen and misshapen. In the half light her skin is ivory. I crouch and put my hand on her leg and feel its cool and its smoothness. I touch my mother's skin and I am her small child again.

A short time passes. 'Does any thing hurt, Mum?'

'No darling.'

'Can you move your limbs, Mum?'

Dad's voice breaks in: 'Mum's not hurt – she didn't fall. She was reaching for the commode chair and she pushed it away instead of holding it still … she just slid gently onto the floor … I couldn't stop her falling …'

Dad's voice subsides. He sits on his bed and holds his head in his hands.

Mum speaks: 'I'm quite comfortable, darling. It's quite a nice floor, really.' Another grin. I look at my mother. Her limbs are splayed and folded beneath and before her like so many pick-up-sticks. I wonder how I will pick them up.

'If you like it on the floor, Mum, would you prefer to stay there until the morning?'

'If you wish, darling.' She extends a hand and pats my face.

I bend and begin to take her weight, my hands beneath her arms. Dad gets up to help but I knock him back because his heart is worn out and failing.

He recoils, recedes and sits down opposite me, his face wrought of grief and care. I feel a pang for my abruptness.

An in-drawing of breath, a grunt and Mum is aloft, her legs a pair of white flags hanging limply beneath her. Her arms are around my neck and we are locked in our accustomed embrace that has become so familiar since she began to suffer a series of strokes.

We know this moment well; each of us knows the sweetness of this slow dance. Neither of us would readily trade it, not even to make Mum whole again.

A moment later Mum is in her bed, covered up, wheezing, speaking breathily, her voice ravaged by stroke and by time: 'Thank you, darling, what a treat!' – and beaming with the simple pleasure of being tucked into her bed.

Dad, contrite, distressed, is saying, 'I am sorry, darling. I hate to disturb you.' And I am saying how pleased I am to come, and how come he didn't speak into the machine when he rang. And Dad says, 'I don't know.'

'*Shabbat Shalom*,' I say, kiss them both goodnight, and go home.

Back home, but not yet in paradise, I sit a while and recall a conversation my friend Lionel reported to me. While driving with my father in the Flinders Ranges, Lionel asks this indestructible old man a singular question: 'What are you afraid of in this life, Myer?'

My dreadnought father has fought all his sixty-seven years as a doctor against illness and injury. Of all diseases, I know that cancer and stroke fill him with terror beyond naming. And I recall, too, Dad confiding to me his fears for Mum: 'I am grateful for every single day that I have her; and I am so frightened of the day that …' He falls silent, his voice drowning in the grief of his imagining.

When Lionel asks his question, Dad looks up and out and away from inside him, and he sees those silent, massive and beauteous living things, so inviting in the outdoors and so treacherous. He answers, 'Falling gum trees.'

The day after the 'fall' Mum and I are alone in the kitchen when she begins to laugh. The sound has a gasping quality. You have to pay close attention to discover whether she is choking again, or simply amused. She laughs louder then tries to speak at the same time.

Her voice is a concerto for bagpipes and windstorm. I lean close, into the teeth of the storm and Mum says, 'When I was on the floor last night, and I couldn't get up, I started to laugh, and I couldn't stop … and Daddy was furious!'

My father the lover II

A visit to Mum's treasure chest reveals a letter written by my father to the grandmother and guardian of the young lady he is soon to marry. I knew the writer, but I have no memory of my great-grandmother 'Gar', the recipient of the letter.

All who knew Gar respected her. It seems she was a phenomenon; my hard-headed Papa saw beyond the accident of Gar's lofty social status and found only praise for her. Even my bluntly spoken Aunty Claire admired this woman who knew no limit to her human reach.

That letter, written in 1942, lies quietly for three score years, a dusty witness to the youthful ardour of my father the lover. It lies entombed in that steel chest from the time of Gar's death in 1948 until this great-grandson comes across it in 2006.

Writer and recipient both pass on, but as their descendant stands among the cobwebs in the garage and reads, Gar is alive to him in all her dignity and wisdom – and Dad is there too, idealistic, confident and ardent.

Passion charges this rather diffident, shy young man with a poetic eloquence. I read the letter and feel the passion. I fear for a moment that I might be a voyeur upon my own father, one who blunders upon a sacred ceremony. Then I feel the honour that the young man pays to the old lady, and the nobility of his sentiments. I see my father standing before me, stripped of his shyness, emotionally naked, beautiful in a new way.

For the second time in her long life, the old lady is about to pass on to a young man a person whom they both love, a person who will become a bride, later a mother, finally a widow. On the first occasion, Gar gives her daughter Marguerite to an adventurer, Cyril Coleman. That man who will become my grandfather is a man of parts, a former pearl diver, a polo player and a concert artist on the one-string violin. He carves hair combs for his bride from tortoise shell and creates jewellery for her with the pearls he wins from the ocean bed. Perhaps, in Gar's eyes, this second young man with his religious ways, who pledges his love to Yvonne, is even more exotic than the pearl diver.

As for the letter writer, he sees the young woman who will be his bride as somehow delicate, perhaps vulnerable. The writer cannot foresee her resilience, how she will survive.

I study photographs of the girl whom my father loves; the bones are strong, but the face is delicate. I cannot stop looking. I see a revelation of the vision that lifts my father and makes him a poet. I too am moved by the seeming frailty in that face that brings out the protector in a man.

The letter writer who becomes my father vows to protect and provide for Yvonne, and he spends the next sixty-three years doing that. Years after his death, he is still her protector and her provider.

He honours the pledge that he makes to the old lady.

Eight

Leaving Leeton

For both Dad and me, leaving Leeton is an amputation from which neither of us fully recovers.

It starts painlessly. Dad brings Dennis and me into the end bedroom for a Serious Talk. He sits us both down on one of the twin beds that he built, then he sits down on the other, facing us. Dad wants to know: 'How would you like to go to Mount Scopus College in Melbourne, and stay with Ruthie and Carmel?'

Ruth and Carmel are our cousins. Their parents are Aunty Claire and Uncle Abe. So it is an easy question to answer; Aunty is the second best cook in the world and Uncle Abe loves us boys as only a man can who lives in a houseful of girls.

'You bet, Dad.'

A short week or two later, Dennis and I are in Melbourne, being interviewed by the Principal. In Leeton, I never heard of a Principal. This man asks me questions: 'How much is nine times seven? How do you spell WONDERING? Can you read me this passage from *The Adventures of Tom Sawyer*?'

My answers must be very good, because the Principal decides that I can go to his school. Or perhaps they are very bad, and he decides I really need to go there.

Aunty Claire takes me to a warehouse in Flinders Lane, where they fit me for a school suit. *A suit!* For SCHOOL! Aunty Claire says it's the school uniform. 'Didn't you have a uniform in Leeton?'

I don't know … I think for a bit. 'They make you wear shoes … most of the time.'

'Well,' says Aunty, 'Mount Scopus is different.'

Dad has gone back to Leeton. This is natural – Leeton is where we live, where my family is. I'm only boarding in Melbourne. I don't realise that I will not be going back to our home. I am unaware that Dad has sold the house and the practice to a new doctor who will take over in six months' time. I have no idea that Mum and Dad will bring Margot and little Barry to join Dennis and me in Melbourne, and that my Leeton days have ended. Dad and Mum imagine that I do understand all this; each presumes that the other told me.

I am nine and a half years old. I arrive in Melbourne a stranger. More than fifty years later I am still a newcomer. Home, that deep place, that landscape of my being, is somewhere else. Home is a town too small for traffic lights. It is a place of dirt roads, a place where children roam freely and their parents have no fears.

There are rivers there lined by huge gum trees, and beaches of coarse white sand. Irrigation canals are everywhere, lined with willows and crawling with yabbies. There are sand hills where you dig caves, and strange sand storms that come suddenly – they darken the sky and for a day the world is upside down. We picnic on the irrigation canals and in summer we swim at the open-air pool from the end of the school day until nightfall.

A few miles out of town is the olive farm and fruit orchard where Uncle Abe lets us help him drive the old truck. In town there is the olive oil and pickling factory that Dad built. Inside are dozens of barrels of pickled olives, hundreds of steel drums of oil, and a mighty furnace roaring with burning wood to create steam for the olive press. Oil runs in a golden-green stream from the crushed olives. The factory has the aroma of warm olive oil. Whenever, in the kitchens of adult life, I smell the aroma of warming olive oil, I feel a wordless sense of pleasure.

We have friends in Leeton. Some live on rice farms and fruit orchards, others are closer. Three doors away from our home is the Leeton Furnishing Company. Behind the shop, in a proud and elegant home on a quaint quadrilateral of land, live our friends the Wanklyns. Johnny Wanklyn, my oldest friend, my best friend, lives in this house, in that town.

When I leave Leeton for Mount Scopus, I will be coming home for the school holidays. I say some *au revoirs* but I make no farewells. Leeton is where my home is, where my life is.

In 1955 I leave, unaware that this is an end.

Ever after, in moments of quietness, often in the pale grey hours of dawn or at the apricot time before nightfall, I inhabit the street-scape of Leeton. The eye in my mind traces the walk along the canal near the pool, or leads me past the school towards the hospital, across the bridge where the bitumen ends and onto the dirt road that leads to our farm at Stony Point.

Twenty-five years later, Johnny Wanklyn reports a recent conversation with a friend. The friend says, 'I've met your sister Julianne, but who's this brother Howard you speak of? I thought your parents only ever had two children …'

'You're right,' says Johnny, 'they did. But Howard Goldenberg is the nearest I'll ever have to a brother.' Hearing this, I reflect that the parting in 1955 leaves deep creases in the feelings and memories of us both.

Every December from 1955 to 1995, my mother receives a letter written in blue ink and a beautiful hand. The writing is from Mum's friend, Dulcie Wanklyn. At this time every year, Dulcie writes cards to her dear ones. Mum's is a letter. Invariably it opens:

> Yvonne Dearest,
> At this time of the year I write Xmas cards to all my loved ones. I know that this is not a religious season for Jewish folk, but I cannot write to all and sundry and

leave out the Goldies. So this is not an Xmas card, but simply my letter to my dear old friend …

With a respect for Jewish sensibilities that is typical (but, in my parents' case, unnecessary), Dulcie substitutes 'X' for 'Christ' in 'Christmas'.

In 1995 the letters stop. Dulcie decides that the standard of her handwriting is not now 'respectable'.

In 1967 I visit Israel and I am moved to discover that here, for the first time since Leeton, I am not a newcomer. In addition to that powerful moment of revelation when the homecoming Jew recognises his place of ancient dream and prayer, something else happens. With my feelings heightened by all these stirrings of folk memory, a landscape looms around me in Galilee, disturbing me strangely. Ambushed, I look up and out and I see gum trees everywhere. They line the narrow country roads linking small country towns. They lead the eye and the mind, hinting at the closeness to water. And there is the Lake Narrandera. This is a district of small farms, of dusty places, of patches of green. I awake in the promised land to a Riverina dreaming.

In my Leeton days, I know few Jewish people. Apart from one-legged Barney, the itinerant hawker who lurches into and out of our lives on his crutches and his bonhomie, the only other Jewish people I know are those who come to stay with us.

Rabbi and Mrs Freedman bring their daughters, Elaine and Ruth. While our parents talk and talk and talk, the young ladies take Dennis and me to the park on *Shabbat* and play with us on the playground equipment. They appear to enjoy our company. Perhaps we are delightful; perhaps in dusty Leeton, Ruth and Elaine are simply deeply bored.

The remainder of our visitors are all relatives. All these people are observant. I conclude that Jewish people are homogeneous; I never dream that a person might be Jewish and not practise the Jewish religion.

Leeton is a good place to be Jewish. Dad and Mum are known to be Jewish and known to be good people, so everyone in Leeton – thousands of people – everyone here holds the expectation that a Jew is a good person. For our part, knowing so many people who are not Jewish and who are good to us (numerous of Mum's friends learn to bake kosher cakes and biscuits and puddings), we absorb the reciprocal belief: the goodness or otherwise of a person does not depend upon religion. (If they bake kosher it is a good sign.)

This is a true thing in our lives that has been an untrue thing in the lives of other Jewish people, people who have fled to Melbourne from Europe. We have never learned to mistrust the world. We have never needed to.

It is in Leeton that we learn how to be Good Jewish Boys. Dad teaches us how. I will learn many things at Mount Scopus but I will not find there any person to inspire me, to teach me the love of Jewishness, to teach me the rules and the skills of a Jewish life, like my father.

Being Jewish is precious; we have *Shabbat* and we have the Festivals. While other people have Christmas and Easter, these are our own special days. One of our festivals is the Festival of Camping Out. Its Jewish name is *Succoth* – it means booths. For eight days we eat outside in a sort of decorated cubby called a *succah*. We eat festive meals in our *succah*, which is the only one in the town. Our friends admire it and wish they had one.

It is in the *succah* that Dad first offers me an aerated drink. It is like cordial but it makes your nose tingle. Evermore I associate that sensation with festive meals.

We eat only kosher food. That means we have to ship our meat to Leeton by train from Melbourne. As a matter of fact, the meat takes two trains. It is taken from the first train at Albury and placed on the second. If there is a rail strike, the meat is delayed and it arrives in Leeton rotten. The strikes are the fault of the Labor Party, Mum says, so she never votes Labor. She almost never eats meat; that must be another way to punish Labor.

The hardest thing about being Jewish in Leeton is not the distance from kosher butcher shops but from kosher ice-cream shops. The closest is one hundred miles away in the small town of The Rock.

Dad likes meat, particularly chicken. He is not fond of rotten meat, however. So Dad does a course in the kosher slaughtering of poultry. The rabbi who teaches him is the same man who circumcises me on the eighth day of my life. Happily he does not confuse his twin vocations.

Dad has no trouble catching on to the technique of ritual slaughter: it's simple surgery taken to an unhealthy length. But I only ever see Dad kill one chook. That chook thanks Dad for his services by running around the yard for a long time. It is the funniest sight of my childhood, but I never see Dad perform an encore.

There are 613 commandments in the Torah, but Dad knows many more than that and he teaches them all to us, especially Thou Shalt Not. Thou Shalt Not Ride your Bike on *Shabbat* is one of the tough ones. Thou Shalt Not Go to the Shops on *Shabbat* is also hard. There are many more. I never have any trouble with the Shalt Nots of Adultery, Idolatry and My Neighbour's Ass.

Thou Shalt Not Pinch is too hard for us. Both Dennis and I pinch money from the drawer in Dad's desk, fairly steadily, over a period of about ten years. It is a highly convenient bank, but you don't want to be caught making a withdrawal.

We have to pray in the morning before we eat. To pray properly as a Jew it is best to read the prayers in Hebrew. So, long before we start school, Dad has taught us to read well in Hebrew.

When, at Mount Scopus, I am called upon to read aloud from biblical or liturgical texts, our daily fare in Leeton, I can read the pants off my classmates. An exacting taskmaster, Dad has trained another perfectionist.

(I discover at Mount Scopus that our Hebrew reading has the wrong accent: we pray in an Anglo-German accent, but modern Hebrew has the accent called *Sephardit*. My old accent is an embarrassment. I feel as if I am barefoot and everyone else is in school uniform.)

There are five *megilloth* – or scrolls – that we read once every year. Each has its distinctive cantillation, and Dad is the master of them all. At *Purim*, Dad reads us one of the classic Jewish texts, the *Megillah* of Esther. It has the classic shape and theme of our festival readings: they tried to kill us, God saved us, let's eat! Dad sings the story of how Esther and Mordechai were God's instruments in saving us from the genocidal Haman. Every time Dad reads the word *Haman*, we have to drown out the sound of that evil name by any means of clamour or racket. It is great fun. After Dad has finished, we eat Haman's ears, crunching hard as we do so. Haman's ears – or *Hamantaschen* – are delicious pastries that Mum bakes once a year.

The most memorable *megillah* is also the most miserable. It is *Eicha*, or Lamentations. It sings of the sack of Jerusalem and the destruction of the Temple by the Babylonians, on the ninth day of the month of Av; and of the Second Temple, by the Romans a few hundred years later, on the self-same date. Unlike the festival readings, there is no happy ending on the ninth of Av: they tried to kill us, they did so, let's fast!

Dad sits us down on the dining room floor. The room is lit only by a small candle. We sit on the thin pink carpet with its patterned fine linear ridges and valleys. The winter evening comes down as Dad reads *Eicha* in a sad melody. He reads from the *Tanach*, the volume of the Bible that he received at his bar mitzvah. The book is heavy, a tome, its pages dyed pink at their edges. There is an English translation (which Dad always pronounces *tran-sell-ation*), and at the end of each chapter, Dad turns from the Hebrew and reads the English to us. He renders the tragic story with all its pain: *They that did feed delicately are desolate in the streets … tender women cooked their own children … who became provender for them …*

As Dad reads on and on, the thin carpet chafes my naked thighs slightly. The feeling is tolerable but, I discover, indelible in my body memory. I cannot hear *Eicha* without recalling that sensation. The ancient tragedies of my people are alive in my flesh, in my ears, and now – in 2006 – in my throat.

This last sensation is a discovery. I am on Elcho Island at *Tisha B'Av*, the ninth day of Av. I have with me a copy of *Eicha* and some candles, but there is no other Jewish person on this island in the Arafura Sea, north-east of Darwin. For the first time in my life, I read – in fact, I sing – *Eicha* aloud. I am amazed to find that I can do a serviceable job; I sing the threnody I learned from my father … that neither of us realised he was teaching.

Leeton is not only a good place to learn Jewish observance, but also to learn to be proud of being Jewish. We learn this from our father. In him we see a person who loves his Jewishness with all his being, absolutely and unapologetically; and at the same time, Dad extends respect to all peoples, all creeds. His self-respect requires no disrespect of the other. My father gives this great gift, this divine gift to his children. It is the gift of seeing the image of the Maker in all of His children.

✳

Dad sends us to Melbourne, then leaves his practice in paradise, solely so we will receive a Jewish education. He does not realise that events in Melbourne will be irrelevant. We will carry our Judaism from Leeton, to Melbourne and beyond; and we can pass it on to our future generations. It is the teaching of our father that we carry.

Dad pays a high price for our move to Melbourne. If the Leeton I carry in my mind is a paradise for children, the Leeton that my father leaves behind is a doctor's paradise. There, Dad is in his element. A country town needs a doctor of many gifts, one who loves his work more than he loves rest. In Dad, Leeton finds a gifted, highly ethical workaholic. He relishes his autonomy. In the country, Dad can deploy all of his gifts and extend them. Dad is the doctor; he will take on anything except eye surgery and complicated cancers.

The people take him to their hearts and he reciprocates. It is a love affair between Dad, medicine and his patients, happily triangulated. Somehow, somewhere, Dad's other loves – his wife, his children, his faith, his hobbies and interests – are all accommodated on Dad's polygon of affections.

When Dad and Mum marry, they move to Leeton 'for two years'. They stay for fourteen. And in leaving, Dad says farewell, a long farewell to the greatness that was. He leaves Leeton without complaint, for his children's Jewish future. Never can he see the greatness that is to follow upon the larger stage that is his life and career in Melbourne. Forty-five years of distinction follow his Leeton days, but Dad alone fails to recognise the greatness that attends him.

With Dad's going, others also suffer amputation. A young woman walks from Dad's surgery, feels dizzy and, a few doors down the street, she faints. She comes to consciousness in The Leeton Furnishing Company, where Mrs Wanklyn is caring for her.

'What happened?' asks Dulcie.

'I just saw my doctor. I'm going to have a baby, and I want him to look after me and my baby. But he told me today he won't be able to. He's going. He's leaving Leeton!'

Leeton is losing one of its organs. People are shocked; most recover. But a few will continue over the next decades to drive to Melbourne, three hundred and fifty dusty miles away, when they are fearful or lost or in some crisis in their lives. They come to see again the doctor who listened, who sewed them up or saved them, the one who understood their grief, their fears, their secrets.

Dad leaves Leeton, embraces his new life in Melbourne and

contributes with distinction in every sphere of his activity. He is busy in Melbourne, profitably occupied, endlessly focusing his ardent mind on new questions, seeking always a worthy task. In the city he is earnest, but he is not carefree. It is only when Dad steps aboard a boat and casts off, or when he drives outside the city limits, that he breathes again the airs and breezes of his joyous prime.

As for me, the moment that I finish my medical studies, I submit to a centrifugal force that flings me from Melbourne to Hobart, to country locums then to Diamond Creek, a village on the green edge of Melbourne.

After a few years, prompted by our own children's need of Jewish schooling and a Jewish community, we too eventually return to the centre.

My temperament is more cheerful than Dad's. Life in Melbourne is not burdensome. It fulfils me deeply. Yet my spirits lift, my steps lighten, I too breathe more deeply whenever I turn my back on the city. I do so often and I ply my trade in remote locums. And often enough, good, generous Annette takes a deep breath of the city air, turns her back on everyone she loves and comes along to keep me company.

✳

In March 2006 my receptionist asks me if I am willing to answer a phone call from Hazel Birbira. This is not a name I know well. Something vibrates in the back rooms of memory and I take the call. As soon as I hear the voice I remember its owner; Hazel lives at Number 10, Wade Avenue, Leeton, New South Wales, with her husband George, the doctor who succeeded the doctor who bought Dad's practice. I meet Hazel only once, on a visit to Leeton with Johnny Wanklyn and all our children in 1984. Hazel shows me over her home, my old home, and it has shrunk amazingly.

After the tour, she shows me the bedroom doorpost. She says, 'We've repainted the house a couple of times since you left. The first time, we found a thin tubular object attached to this lintel. We took it down and when we prised it open we found some parchment with Hebrew writing. George is Lebanese; he recognised it. He said, "It's the sign of a Jewish house. It is a sacred object for Jewish people."'

Hazel interrupts her narrative as she leads me now to the front door. 'And here,' Hazel points to the lintel where I recognise our old *mezuzah* covered in coats of paint, 'here is another one. When we saw this second one we knew it was holy, so we let it be.'

Hazel has sad news. George has died – of stroke, heart attack, pneumonia – 'and of overwork.' Then she adds: 'For the first time in eighty-four years there is no doctor living and practising at 10 Wade Avenue. Would you like to come back and work in Leeton?'

Nine

My Father's Compass

When my father teaches me the rudiments of navigation, and the distinction between magnetic north and true north, he is unwittingly establishing the framework in my mind by which I might distinguish integrity from expediency. The example of Dad's life provides his children with a compass that will steer us truly through the time ahead.

Although I never have occasion to steer a boat anywhere near the poles, I discover that my father's compass is proof against the confusing tides and troubled waters in which I wash up at different times in my life.

Somehow my prolonged childhood comes to an end. I become a husband, a doctor then a father. Over the same period my own father retires from his roles as chairman and managing director of Howard Goldenberg. He withdraws unobtrusively and tactfully, some time during my late teenage years. It is only afterwards that I notice.

Although always anxious to perfect his children, ever fearful of a fateful error in my life, at some stage Dad must gain confidence in me – or does he simply weary of the task of control?

If there is a particular moment when Dad makes his decision to 'retire', it might be in December 1964. It follows a meeting between Dad and the Professor of Anatomy at my medical school.

I have just completed my second year in which the sole examinable subject is Anatomy. During my oral examination, the Professor listens to the examiner's questions, sucking thoughtfully on his pipe, adding a few questions of his own, attending courteously to my stumbling and inadequate responses. At length my half hour is up. As he moves away he makes the following quiet observation: 'Mr Goldenberg, I believe that over the past twelve months, you and I have been studying the anatomy of two quite distinct species.'

Thankful that the ordeal had ended, grateful for the mildness of the Prof's tone, deaf to its ironic obliquity, I am only dimly aware that the remark does not augur well.

When the results are published, my name is not among the Passes; nor is it among those with a Credit, a Distinction or a High Distinction. Nor have I won the prize for top marks. Instead, I am awarded a Supplementary Examination, a second chance. The exam will be in three months' time. I will have to study Anatomy through the long summer break if I still want to become a doctor. I jump at it.

Dad comes home and tells me he has met with the Professor. I am shocked, humiliated. I don't know what to say. Dad says: 'I went there to ask him what I could do to help you. Do you know what his reply was?'

Amazed still, dazed by the idea of the conjunction of these two huge planets that determine my fate, I have no idea what the Professor might have said. 'What did he say, Dad?'

'He said, "Dr Goldenberg, surely you realise that you've had no control over your son since he was fourteen years old."'

I had been dismayed at Dad going to see the Prof. Now dismay gives way to indignation; what does the Prof know about my father and me? Nothing!

Then a novel thought, a worrying idea: if Dad hasn't been at the helm of my recent years, who has? Surely I haven't? Shocked, I try to absorb this radical notion. The realisation will take some years. Quickly I slide into anxious denial. I want to reassure my father that his place in my life is secure. 'It's not true, Dad!' But Dad seems to accept the news quite readily.

Years pass, pleasant years in which I become a peer of my peerless father – not a clown, not an infant, not automatically wrong when I differ from him. I enjoy his respect. His occasional compliments take me by surprise: 'You've been wiser than I have, Howard, to take holidays, to enjoy leisure. I scarcely ever did …'

'You are a very good father, Howard, a far better father than I ever was …'

And – disconcertingly – 'Howard, I want you to be my doctor.'

How could I possibly manage such an insubordinate patient? How would Dad cope with an insubordinate doctor? I don't deserve this honour; neither of us deserves this.

But this warm feeling, this basking in unexpected sunshine reminds me of my bar mitzvah. Dad's gift to me on that occasion is characteristically unpretentious, a bit on the modest side. It is a volume of the Five Books of Moses. He inscribes the flyleaf with his Parker fountain pen. The writing is fine and clear. Dad has made an uncharacteristic effort to make his words legible:

> To Howard,
> Who has proven himself worthy of his heritage.

Dad's words are spare, hardly effusive, but even at thirteen years of age, I begin to sense their significance. (Twenty-eight years later my own son will prepare as I did, and distinguish himself at his bar mitzvah; and I will understand more fully my father's mind as he sat down to write those words.)

There is a little more to the short inscription:

> … from his proud and loving
> Daddy.

Naturally Dad loves me. That is one of the foundations of my being. But there in blue ink are the words *proud and loving*. Proud

– of me! The words are a private reward for two years of daily practice under Dad's perfecting eye, seven hundred days of straining to please him, of frequent stumbling and painful imperfection. After two years of daily bruising as one perfectionist tried to raise another, here is my certificate, my validation. Now *proud* stands with *loving*, a foundation for my adult being.

In our growing up, it was hard for us children to win Dad's praise. Even his approval was scarce. Did Dad fear we would become complacent if we were overfed with compliments? I am certain that my brothers, my sister and I all hungered for Dad's approval; that, far from overfed, we were competing for scraps; and the competition between us gave enduring shape to our rivalry.

Even as a grown-up, whenever I hold a different opinion from Dad's, I wrestle strenuously with him. It's quite spontaneous. I am testing myself, compulsively, trying still to prove myself. Dad pays me the compliment of never yielding in any of these arguments. In the decades of our adult wrestling, he never concedes a fall.

Whenever I drive a car or manoeuvre a boat with Dad as a passenger, he remains more than generous with his advice. And the advice is imperious, inviting no dissent. I am well into my fifties, but Dad still knows best. Yet throughout, it is still my way, still my pleasure to show deference and honour to my father.

After my father dies, I find plentiful occasion to honour my father in memory. His life illuminates my path. Moments of beauty that I shared with Dad visit me and remind me of gifts he gave me. I see an empty sea, silent at dawn; I hear the sound of classical music, or my nephew practising for his bar mitzvah – the distinctive melody is Dad's. The finesse and fidelity of the boy's rendition, these were Dad's; that sweet melodious voice reminds me of Dad's light tenor.

My children are now adults. I recognise in their lives moments of light. Here is endeavour, here persistence; there is courage, there humble nobility. When I see these things, it seems to me they too are heading north. Autonomously. And they honour their own father and their mother – boisterously – with a wrestling quality my father might recognise from his Sunday mornings with his own children.

I know where my kids are facing.

There are moments in my work when the second-rate tempts me. It's just an ordinary moment: an easier way presents itself, winks at me, a lazy short cut. It wouldn't be fatal to my patient, just expedient for me. A lazy antibiotic here, a dodgy medical certificate there. How much harm can it do? A slack physical examination, a flaccid mental effort – who will know?

The memory of father's way is immediately with me: he would not compromise here. In the event, I might choose the easier path. And I find that I can choose without guilt, and still feel grateful to Dad for the knowledge of choice, grateful still for his example.

In religious observances Dad would allow himself no latitude, but I negotiate with myself. Perhaps I'll allow myself to be unpunctual for this synagogue service; perhaps I will be less pedantic about that dietary law; or I might ask – is this observance mandatory or merely customary? And yet, a custom never feels 'mere' to me if it is one that Dad cherished, a custom received by him and passed down to me.

Dad built many fences around the Law, anxious never to break it by accident. In my childhood he was a boundary rider, checking on my fences as well as his own. How high, how many will be the fences that I build?

All these are choices I can make quite freely. Long before I was ready to be free, Dad set me free.

The day came when a man smashed his way into my life and work. He said, '*I will kill you.*' The man was menacing: he described the means at his disposal. He evinced a terrible malignity of purpose. What would I do? How would I react? I saw my father, saw his courage. Perhaps I would find courage too.

Dad's opinions were ever his own. He never bought cheap popularity by conforming with a majority. Late in Dad's life, with the world turning its face against tolerance, against dissent, against pluralism, Dad seemed to be moving left against a relentless rightward tide. More likely, he simply held course. His own path through a long life remained straight and clear. Dad stayed so faithful to his own north that I see it constantly, luminous always, through the light and the occasional dark. I am never lost.

Dad gave me a blessing he never received from his own father: *Go your own way.* And I do. Most often my way is the same as my father's. I am not embarrassed to walk in his footsteps. And always – clear, shining, showing a path ahead – I see Dad's way: True North.

Waiting

My father never wasted time. Ever on the move, he was always one step ahead of time. But now time lays him waste. Dad lies in his hospital bed, his eyes not quite closed. Does he see me? I stand in front of the bed and wait.

I have come here directly from the airport. Sixteen days ago, Dad's health was stable and I flew away, a climate refugee, to Alice Springs and far north Queensland. In Alice, I ran the half-marathon and visited the places Dad and I had enjoyed together a year ago. In Port Douglas I ran the length of the beach, recalling my father's remarkable stamina during our visit two years before. Despite his nearly ninety years, Dad found the strength then for daily walks of up to four miles, ending at the nude beach. He enjoyed the sea, the sun and the feminine scenery.

During the current trip I would talk with Dad on the phone. Repressing my anxiety for him, I'd tell him I loved him. Dad, quite untroubled, replied simply, 'I love you, Howard.'

There are months of pain. We watch our warrior father swim against a tide that has to overwhelm him. We see him rail angrily at his failing body, girding himself daily for lone battle. Dad pushes away offers of help. He locks us out and stands his siege alone.

My brothers, my mother and I are all witness to Dad's losing battles. I feel I must do something. Imagination fails me and, by some sort of reflex, I give practical advice. I need to fix things. I feel irritated at Dad's independence. (Why won't Dad inform his doctor of these events? Why does he always know better than everyone else? Why doesn't he allow us to help him?)

I am a bully, pressing this proud man to swallow his pride and accept help. Sometimes, though, I find kindness and patience, and respond without judgment.

'Have you had a bad night Dad?'

He sits at the kitchen table, leaning far backward in his chair, bracing his joints. His reply comes through teeth gritted against the pain: 'Not so good.'

I work my way carefully through the inventory of things that aren't so good – the frozen shoulder, the gouty foot, the spinal stenosis, the failing heart, the failed kidneys, the diabetes that chews away at his peripheral nerves so he can no longer discern the ends and edges of his body. And the loss of balance. The semi-circular canals deep inside his head have forgotten which way is up and they fling Dad repeatedly to the ground, tearing off sheets of his skin, leaving his thin blood to ooze into pools and trails to be found later by his distressed family.

Most days, most of these things aren't so good.

'Does it get on top of you, Dad?'

A pause. The voice is tired, ragged at its edges: 'If this is my life from here on, I don't want to go on …'

Another pause, longer this time. I get up from my chair, walk over to Dad and hold his battered head against my belly. At times like these I try prepare my mother for an end: 'Heart failure is dangerous, Mum. People die of it.'

Mum takes my hand and, stroking it, speaks kindly to me: 'I know Daddy might die, darling. That's what happens to old people …' She looks up at me, into me, searching my innocence. I am in my late middle years; she lost her own parents in her early teens – is her son ready for this?

My mother is trying to protect *me!*

Three days ago my father was seated in the kitchen with my mother, when her carer announced she would make them some lunch. But Dad saw food preparation as his prerogative – was he not host to the carer, and carer to his wife? Acting on ancient reflex, he sprang to his feet, lost balance and fell heavily onto the back of his head. He knocked himself out and landed in hospital.

Unlike my father, I am not punctual. I return now to Melbourne, three days late, bearing my load of anxiety and guilt.

Apart from his breathing, Dad is quite still. His stillness is ominous; old people lying still for too long develop pneumonia and die. It was Dad who first taught me that pneumonia is 'the old man's friend'. I look at my father, lying so motionless, awaiting a visit from the old man's friend.

The words of another old physician come indistinctly to mind. Writing in *The Story of San Michele*, Axel Munthe sees Death as his professional opponent: 'I have for so long been wrestling with my old adversary, and one by one I have seen him take the people I laboured to save …'

I look at my father. He breathes regularly, but his exhalation is laboured. His blue lips balloon outwards with each expiration. Nowadays expiration signifies the date you sniff suspiciously at the milk or renew your credit card. When something expires time is up. I watch my father breathing and I think about expiration.

Dad's voice breaks into my thoughts. The voice is scarcely audible. The words are slurred. 'What time is it?'

'It's noon, Dad.'

Dad's eyes widen in surprise, then close again. He sleeps.

I think about Dad and time. Apart from his habitual punctuality, Dad's focus at work lay on matters of time. Between December 1933 and June 2002, Dad might have conducted three-quarters of a million medical consultations and I am confident he interrogated every single patient about time: 'When did this symptom start? And when did that symptom start? When were you last quite well? How long is it between the pains?'

I look at my father, a sleeping lion. At this and every subsequent visit, he is curious to know the time. But time, his old pacesetter, is eluding him. He hears me tell him the time, but he doesn't quite grasp it and it slips away. Then he closes his eyes and he goes where time is a stranger.

Dad was born in 1910. I am reminded of the year of his birth whenever I drive through Kew Junction. There, set in a tiny kite-shaped patch of lawn, is a non-memorial to Raoul Wallenberg, the Swedish diplomat who saved thousands of Hungarian Jews from the Nazis. When the war ended, Wallenberg was snatched away by the Soviets and he disappeared into the Gulag. He never emerged. Sightings were reported but never confirmed. Decades passed, communism fell and Wallenberg became a cause célèbre, but with the passing of the millennium and his ninetieth birthday, Wallenberg passed from silent question mark to deep and utter silence. The monument in Kew comprises the bronze bust of a slight man, below which we read: *Raoul Wallenberg, 1910–.*

The bust rests on a beam which is massive and strong at one end, but broken off at the other. It is a non-memorial because it does not reach finality.

No one on the face of this earth knows Wallenberg's fate. The man who never came back might yet live. My father, his contemporary, leaves us and returns. In his absences, Dad's mouth moves, framing words we cannot hear. Perhaps he visits Wallenberg while he is absent.

Hello, Raoul.
Hello, Myer.

Are you free yet, Raoul?

Not yet. And you, Myer?

Not yet. Not yet. Soon, perhaps …

I wait and watch my Dad. He lies and awaits his fate.

When I visit Dad at lunchtime on the following day, he hasn't eaten his breakfast. The nurse tells me he won't eat until he has prayed. I ask Dad if he would like to pray with me. Then his rabbi turns up. Even though the rabbi is only half Dad's age, he is Dad's friend. He is blessed with the necessary sense of humour.

Dad is weak, deeply drowsy and too confused to recite the entire service. But if he doesn't pray, he won't eat; and if he doesn't eat, he'll weaken further. The kindly rabbi recommends a shortened version.

I lead Dad through the essentials: *Hear, O Israel, the Lord our God, the Lord is one.* Then I recall the special psalm for the current period of repentance. It is one of Dad's favourites and one of my own. We start: *The Lord is my light and my salvation …*

After a few lines Dad is asleep and I am reading to myself. I come to the sentence that always disturbed me as a child: *Yea, even if my father and my mother forsake me, the Lord will gather me up …* As a boy I couldn't imagine life without my father, and I don't want to imagine it now. I am glad that I have to go back to work, grateful that the rabbi is feeding my Dad the fruit salad and yoghurt I had brought him.

The next day Dad is stronger, the following day stronger still. He sits out of bed and attacks his kosher meal with his plastic fork. The meal comprises rice and fish that look older and tougher than my father, but Dad is intent on eating it.

A doctor comes to visit Dad. He is young and good looking. With his brilliant smile and his shock of dark brown hair, he reminds me of photographs of the young Dr Goldenberg, circa 1933. The doctor has come to assess Dad for the purposes of his possible rehabilitation.

'Hello, Dr Goldenberg, I am Dr Sgro.'

'Nice to meet you.' (The voice is weakened by head injury and muffled by its passage through a mouthful of fish. I speak fish passably well, and translate for Dr Sgro.)

'I have come to see how we can get you back to the condition you were in before you came to hospital.'

'Complete fantasy.'

'What do you mean?'

'It might be a fantasy. I might not be able to get back home.'

'What would *you* like, Dr Goldenberg?'

'I want to go back home.'

'Good. Let's see if you can. Who is the Prime Minister?'

'If you don't know, I won't tell you.'

They both laugh.

Dr Sgro asks Dad to subtract seven repeatedly from one hundred until he reaches sixty-five. This Dad does with perfect accuracy. He loses me at eighty-six. Absurdly, I feel a little bit proud, and I bet Dad does too. I go back to work in better spirits.

Dad has been a faithful Jew. He has kept the Sabbath and the festivals at their appointed times, always zealous to honour them, anxious to start them early and terminate them late, never to cheat them of a single minute.

It is now Saturday morning, five days after my return. Dad and I have long had a Sabbath routine together – I join him at the early service in the synagogue across the road from my parents' home. Dad is punctual, I arrive late. By the time I arrive he is absorbed in his prayers and, rather than start a conversation, I lean over him and kiss his bald head in wordless greeting. The congregation pretends to be scandalised by my indecorum, but they are happy to see us play out our little ritual of affection. After the service we always go back to Dad's place for the rituals of *kiddush* – a sip of wine for Mum, a shot of whiskey for Dad, then coffee and cakes for all.

Today I have walked six kilometres to the hospital to help Dad say the Sabbath prayers and to recite *kiddush*. The rabbis say that the Sabbath is a sample of paradise. I want to give Dad his weekly sample.

'Good *Shabbos*, Dad.'

Dad looks up, eyes wide.

'It's *Shabbos*, Dad. I've come to say the prayers with you.' Dad's wide eyes betoken surprise, or something quite beyond my knowing. He makes no response to the news of the Sabbath and the invitation to pray.

He is in pain. His sore old right shoulder is calcified and frozen; he is terrified of moving it. And now his left elbow is on fire. His joints give him no peace. He can't move without pain. The nurses tell me he is confused and angry. He won't let them move him or help him to the shower or toilet.

Dad is lying at an awkward angle in his bed. I bend over him and put my arm behind him, at a safe distance from his sore shoulder. Very slowly, very carefully I take his weight. He screams in pain – or the fear of pain: 'Let me go! You're hurting me!'

As carefully as I can, I return Dad to his previous posture. He speaks. His voice is low, almost a moan. It comes from a long way away: 'I am sick and tired of these people.'

'What do you mean, Dad?'

'They won't let me go the toilet. They won't let me go and shower. Help me Howard.'

But I know that Dad cannot stand. Since his fall a week ago he has been in a stupor, emerging from time to time from his concussion, conversing briefly then falling again into stupor. He cannot stand, he cannot walk, but in his memory he is the active young ninety-two-year-old of a few weeks ago. That youth took himself to the toilet, showered himself, and even – by dint of frail, failing muscles and unfailing will – cared for my crippled mother. Now he is a caged lion, restless, irritable in confinement, frustrated that 'these people' will not allow him to exercise his will.

'Get out of the way,' he says. 'I am going to the shower.'

'Dad, you can't.'

'Don't say stupid things. I know what I can do. Get out of my way.'

'Dad, I can't let you.'

Dad makes a face and lies back. He takes a breath and speaks. His voice is still low, but his speech is clear now and his manner intense. 'Your visit is giving me no pleasure!' He lies back and breathes. He breathes in, blows out. I watch him as he exhales. He falls asleep.

Raoul, do they torture you too?

Not any more, Myer. Eventually, we pass where torture cannot touch us.

The eyes open. Dad thrusts his leg out of the bed. My torso obstructs it. Dad reaches towards me, grasps my shoulder and pulls me to one side to clear his progress. He leans out of the bed about to fall, but I restrain him. I hold his thrusting arm which is stained dark where the thin blood of extreme age has pooled and bruised the skin. Surgical dressings of pristine white form a patchwork on the browns and the purple. I take Dad's limb by one of its few uninjured places and as gently as I can, push it back into bed.

Dad is in a frenzy now: 'Let go of me! Get out of my way!' He raises his arm and makes to thump me, then pulls back at the last moment. The old lion, injured, is snarling at his cub.

He lies back. I don't know how to comfort him.

Silence.

Raoul, why are you here?

What do you mean?

I mean, what did you do? Did you do wrong?

Myer, all I did was try to save some lives.

Me too, Raoul. I don't understand.

Thirty-five years ago I came to this hospital as a medical student. I spent three years here. The day I arrived I saw death for the first time.

Thirty years before that, my father had been a medical student here and later, a house medical officer. I grew up hearing his stories of those years. He told me of a young man who had fallen from a roof onto his outstretched arm, fracturing his radius and ulna. Dad examined him, x-rayed the limb and took him to theatre, where he reduced and set the fractures. Dad was pleased, the young man was happy, but at the ward round next morning, the consultant was not. Dad had carried out a meticulous examination, but had not performed a rectal examination on this otherwise healthy young carpenter.

'Why didn't you do the rectal examination?'

'There wasn't enough time, sir.'

'Well, do it now!'

'Yes sir. Could I have a glove please, nurse?'

'No glove. You should have thought of it earlier. Do it without!'

Sixty-five years later, Dad is in the Alfred Hospital again and, once again, he is in the poo. A voice rustles in the quiet room: 'What time is it, Howard?'

'Dad, it's ten o'clock.'

He looks around, searching the room for clues. 'Is it morning, or ...?'

'Yes, Dad, it's ten in the morning.'

'I've got to get up and go to the clinic.'

'It's *Shabbos* today, Dad. I've come to do the prayers with you and give you wine and bread.'

Dad is amazed: 'Is it *Shabbos*?'

'Yes Dad.'

He allows me to recite *kiddush* and lets me give him a sip of wine. I tell Dad I'll get him a cappuccino. I ordered and paid for it before the *Sabbath* so Dad would be able to enjoy this little luxury. He loves coffee. He especially loves the luxury of the froth. I hurry down the seven flights of stairs to pick up his coffee, then climb up again in a cautious canter, trying not to disturb the froth.

'Dad, here's some coffee for you, steaming hot.'

He shakes his head.

'Dad, it's a cappuccino. I think you'll like it.'

The rustling from an old dry throat takes shape: 'You know I'm not allowed to drink coffee.'

'No Dad, I don't know that. You like cappuccino – try it.'

'The dietitian says I can't.' Dad's speech is a low sound, indistinct. I lean forward to hear as he strains to produce a voice. The words are an irritable crackle borne on a zephyr. 'Why consult an expert if you're not going to follow her advice?'

There follows a debate. Did the dietitian really rule out coffee? Will it really harm him? Is Dad certain it will raise his potassium? Doesn't he know that his potassium has fallen to a safe level?

The struggle is uneven and unfair. And unavailing. I am badgering my weak and confused father. His fragments of voice throw up the wrong words. Dad produces 'cocoa' instead of coffee, and 'magnesium' where he means potassium. Our conversation degenerates rapidly from cross-purposes to cross words.

Presently Dad's nurse, desperate to find some way of helping this distressed old man, finds a dietitian and interrogates her. Yes, the patient may safely have a couple of coffees a day.

But Dad will not drink. The coffee sits in its cup, cools and loses its froth. Two days ago, Dad drank his cappuccino with relish and a clear mind. I wonder whether he has drunk his last coffee; whether that pleasure, like so many others, is lost to him now.

Dad sleeps fitfully, crying out as he makes small unguarded movements in his sleep. I lean forward and kiss my father's bald head, then run – Sabbath laws and heavy clothes notwithstanding – as fast I can, down the seven flights of stairs and all the way home. The distance is six kilometres and it is not enough.

An end

Our waiting comes to an end. Four days after our Sabbath struggles; twelve days after Dad falls at home and hurts his head; fifty-seven years and nine months and two days after he becomes my father, Dad dies. It is too soon.

> Because I could not stop for Death,
> He kindly stopped for me …

The last four days are a dream during which my father awakens to the sounds of loving voices, then sleeps. We visit by day and by night. Time blurs. Coffee and prayer carry me through. My children and my wife are my stay. Friends and family are everywhere about me and I need never be alone with my thoughts and fears.

Humming with activity later and later into the night, dizzily doing practical things, I remain awake until I am too tired even for fear of darkness, then I fall deep into sleep. When I was small, Dad would come into the bedroom as the night drew around us and help us recite the bedtime prayer. While Dad was there, the dark did not frighten me.

Four days. After ninety-two years there remain four days for goodbyes. Many are those who come to say goodbye.

My friend Lionel comes with me to visit Dad. Dad is glad to see him, as always. Lionel says, 'Rita and I are going to Kenya tomorrow – is there anything you'd like me to bring you from Africa, Myer?'

Dad appears to think for a while. In the silence, I wonder whether he has fallen asleep. Then his voice travels across the room and reaches us with his answer: 'A kangaroo tail.'

Lionel laughs. He thinks Dad has made a joke. I *think* that I think Dad is making a joke. Or has he perhaps confused Lionel's imminent trip to Africa with the visit we three made last summer to the Flinders Ranges?

Very early next morning I drive Lionel and Rita to the airport. We detour briefly to the Alfred so I can drop off some home-cooked food for Dad. The night nurse has been scathing about the pap they give Dad in hospital. As I enter Dad's darkened room, I hear his voice. The sound is a low continuous rattle. It sounds empty of meaning and intent, and it unnerves me. I put the food next to his bed, wanting to turn and leave without speaking. Then scruple gets the better of me and I tell Dad that I've brought food, adding, 'Annette made it for you, Dad.'

When I leave the room, the rattle of my father's voice takes shape: 'Thank everyone for me. You are all very kind.'

We drive to the airport where Rita and Lionel embrace me tenderly. The serious look on their faces tells me that they do not expect to see Dad again.

As I come and go over these last days, I encounter friends and relatives. Here is my oldest cousin, Big Barry; on his arm is my ancient aunt, Aunty Doreen. Her skeleton is an articulated collection of painful parts, but pain will not stop her walking these long corridors to see Myer.

When we both were boys, Big Barry was breathtakingly naughty and, naturally, he was my hero; now he is a man of mature years. Man and boy, he and Dad maintained an improbable friendship. We meet as he emerges from the hospital. He tries to speak, then he shakes his head and his handsome face collapses.

Here are Dad's mates from the synagogue. These men are much younger than Dad but they are his friends nonetheless. In their intimate congregation, Dad is part father figure, part mascot. One of the friends makes a sad little joke: 'Myer – when you come to *shule* next *Shabbat*, you can lead the service.' The speaker is a great bull of a man, one of many who loved to trade boisterous insults with Dad, but now he is tender. He falls into silence as he sits by the bed, rising at length and leaving in tears.

More cousins come. My cousins, with whom I was ever wont to joke and clown, are solemn now. They stand at the brink of the unknowable, stand silently, holding one another, looking at their uncle, looking beyond to their own father who made this journey only a few years before.

Do they have any notion how deeply their presence nourishes me?

A few years ago, when their father was dying, he asked his pious brother-in-law, Myer, to read favourite prayers and psalms aloud from the cherished prayer book he received at his bar mitzvah. As Dad read, the two old men were moved to tears. As Dad recounted it to me, he wept again.

Every day, Dad's young doctor makes time to talk with me. He does this kindly and tactfully, never hinting at the competing demands upon his time and attention. Surely Dad is his oldest patient, surely the least saveable. But Dr David Campbell, with his long pony tail and his natural courtesy, treats Dad with loving care.

This afternoon David reports a new diagnosis: 'Your father has an infected elbow. The skin is very inflamed and we think the infection might go deeper – perhaps into the joint itself. We'd like to put antibiotics into the drip. Perhaps even include Gentamycin – if his kidneys can tolerate it.'

This is food for immediate thought. Dad has always hated the way hospitals prolong death; to him, over-treating the incurable is a grotesque unkindness. I feel the same, and it falls to me to express Dad's wishes. However, I have an uncomfortable sense that another of Dad's children would draw the line more widely. Bluntly, another might want to *do everything* to save his life, while I want to spare him unnecessary suffering. And (if I reflect honestly) spare myself as well. But an infected elbow – antibiotics cure things like that. And the injections given into the drip won't cause Dad any extra pain.

'OK, David. Go ahead. And thanks for the call.' After each of our conversations I feel glad that my father's doctor is just like the doctor my father used to be. Excepting for the ponytail; Dad would hate that.

When I was a junior medical student, Dad used to take me into the hospital next door, to see him deliver a baby or to assist him in the operating theatre. I was struck as much by his unhurried gracefulness as by the miracle of birth itself. In the hurly burly of delivery he was calm and calming.

Now that his life is ending, I recall my father in those moments when he helped life begin. I recall it all and, in the pride of remembering, sweet tears salt my eyes and throat.

My son-in-law wants to help. 'Anything, Howardo,' he says in his Argentine accent. 'Anything' turns out to be a hospital visit with me at 6.00 a.m., an hour which violates the Latin constitution. But as the sun rises on this crisp morning, Pablo is there. In his elegant suit he looks expensive and Latin and very smooth.

We go to the ward together. Here are the night nurses I've met during these vigils – the older Dutch one, and the younger girl from Tasmania. It was the elder of the two who, a couple of nights earlier, had commanded me to bring Dad food from home. 'Hospital meals are not good,' she barked, 'and the kosher ones are maybe the worst. Bring your father things he likes to eat.'

Jodie is the name of the younger nurse. She sees Dad's three sons come early and late. She receives overseas calls from our sister every day, at first from New York, later from Budapest. One night, as I sit at Dad's bedside, she says, 'I want to have a family like yours.'

At first I don't understand. Then she says, 'A family that cares. Your brothers and sister, and your mother, and all the nephews and nieces and grandchildren, even your father's sisters-in-law – you all come, you phone, you look after your father and your mother. Not all families are like that. You are a tribe.'

The two nurses have forty years of experience, but all those years are not enough to protect them against the night they have just passed with Dad. 'Your father is in pain. He won't let us help him. He doesn't let us touch him. He is moaning and crying and angry and we cannot help …' The tough Dutch staccato is delivered at high volume but it doesn't conceal the angst of a carer unable to care.

Jodie's softer voice says, 'He needs a wash and a change, but he's too upset … he seems frightened.'

When I go into Dad's room, something smells terrible. His bed-clothes are tangled around him. He lies trapped in them. He moans and nurses his elbow. It is all familiar, a re-run of *Shabbat*. This time I am not so timorous. I secure his elbow by holding Dad firmly by his upper arm, then I roll him over onto his side. He cries out in fear and I tell him he is safe. Before I can ask for help, Pablo bends and supports Dad as I free him from his entanglement and ease him out of his gown. Now the source of the smell is revealed. Dad's infected elbow is a volcano that has erupted. Pus issues from the inflamed skin. The fiery skin and the foul liquid are like an accusation.

Jodie approaches the bed, facing across the room towards the window and the distant sea, away from Dad's exposed body. She wants to spare him embarrassment. She hands me something warm. It is a package of large soft cloths that she has heated up in a microwave. They are like the warm moist towels you get after sitting cooped up for twenty hours on a plane from the other side of the world. I use them to wash Dad all over, enjoying the luxury of them. Crouching, stroking my naked father with the towels, intimate with him and with Pablo, I am deeply happy.

Afterwards Pablo drives, not to work but back home – back to his wife and his baby son. He asks Rachel for a hug and she holds him long and strong, while Pablo recalls his own father, dying alone and too soon, on the opposite side of the world.

During the day, Dad's great-niece comes and feeds him some soup. She is doing the final year of her medical course here at the Alfred. She has been visiting Dad – sometimes three times a day – and feeding him. This time he coughs after only a few spoonfuls and the soup is put aside.

Later David Campbell calls, our second conversation today. 'Your father has taken a turn for the worse,' he says, and the moment is here. I have been preparing for this moment since Dad turned seventy; three score years and ten is the term of our biblical warranty, and once Dad passed that I started to prepare.

My preparation consisted of asking myself was I at peace with my father, and was I ready to say goodbye. The answers were always yes to the first and no to the second … until recently, when the answers were reversed.

David is giving me the facts: 'Your father's blood pressure and oxygen saturations fell quite sharply. He was blue and coughing.' I hear all the data but I am sitting quietly at the far corner of my mind, facing the one large truth.

'We did a chest x-ray. It shows consolidation in the entire middle lobe of his right lung.' Consolidation. That's pneumonia. The old man's friend is here at last.

'We're giving him oxygen and his colour has improved. And some morphine – to keep him comfortable …'

Morphine will make Dad breathe more comfortably. He won't feel fear or the distress of shortness of breath. And it will suppress his cough too. It will also make his breathing weaker. David knows that I understand the significance of morphine. Amen to morphine. Amen and amen.

My older brother Dennis arrives, bringing with him an elderly rabbi. The rabbi is one of the many holy types who are drawn to the devout maverick who is my father. They love his scepticism and his quirky wit. And they respect his integrity.

'Dad, I've brought a friend.'

Dad opens his eyes. He smiles a wide smile, raises himself up in his bed and clasps the hands of his old friend.

'Would you like me to pray with you Myer? Some psalms?' The psalms are the poetry of the hero-king David, in his scrapes with death and his quest for salvation. They are the poetry of love and trust.

Ask Dad what he thinks of poetry and he will make a face. He claims he doesn't get it. But he loves the psalms, as he loves all song.

The rabbi reads aloud some of Dad's favourites. His voice is deep as the earth. The Hebrew words and the English translation are part of the familiar furnishings of Dad's mind. The rabbi's reading is a gift, a walk through his old treasures, given now to my father just as he gave them to my uncle. The rabbi concludes with a hymn:

> Into Your hand
> I consign my spirit
> In my time of sleep
> And when I awaken;
> And with my spirit, my body too –
> The Lord is with me,
> I will not fear.

Anyone who has attended synagogue with my father knows how he loves this closing hymn. While others in *shule* are getting up from their seats to go home, chatting with neighbours, putting away prayer books, Dad sits and sings stoutly to the end. He sings every single word. The final couplet – 'The Lord is with me / I will not fear' – is Dad's credo. When he was a small boy it was his incantation in the dark. It is getting dark now. The rabbi closes – 'I will not fear.'

Grandchildren come. They face the appalling reality of a man stripped of his heat and human powers. There, in that bed, lies flesh of their flesh, bone of their bone – wordless, heedless and ravaged. Their grandfather's breathing is punctuated by spasms of coughing. He makes a groaning sound as his drowning chest struggles to clear itself. The sound arrests us. It comes from the brain's last centre of resistance and it chills all who hear it.

The grandchildren stand around the bed, some with spouses. In the silence between coughing fits, they search for words to bridge the widening gulf. They do not find them. They stand until it is time to leave, when they say, 'Goodbye Grandpa. We're going now.' And they go.

My brother has brought his daughter and his son, the youngest grandchildren. The girl's face is wet. Tears fall continually, running down her wet cheeks, the large drops gathering in a line along her jaw as she stands and strokes her grandfather's bald head. Her eyes gaze as she leans over the bed, as if searching for the person she knew as Grandpa.

Her younger brother carries his reactions inside him. His face betrays nothing. He stands further back and he takes everything in. Like his grandfather he seems to value calm.

Dad's kidneys close down. He enters a stupor now, not eating, not drinking, but no longer in pain. Voices reach him in his far places. His eyes flick open and search, then close before they can find the speaker.

I call my sister who lives in New York. She is visiting Hungary with her husband who is running a suicide prevention program somewhere up the Danube.

'Margot, Dad's kidneys have failed. He seems to be comfortable, but they suspect he has pneumonia. I think time is short …'

Margot says, 'I'll book the first flight.'

It is night in Hungary and all the airlines are asleep, so Margot calls the States and secures a convoluted passage home via Paris, New York and Los Angeles. At the earliest, she will arrive in sixty hours, but there are no guarantees.

My older brother has returned with our mother. Dad shows no sign that he knows of Mum's presence. She sits and holds the hand of her bridegroom of sixty-one years, while he sleeps. She stays a long time and, when she leaves, he still has not reacted.

'Goodbye, darling,' she says softly.

Later, I ask Mum whether she woke Dad to say her goodbyes. 'He was asleep, darling. I didn't want to disturb him.'

Forty years ago Mum and Dad took into their home a young doctor from Leeds. He stayed for half a year and we wished it were longer. That once-young doctor comes now to the hospital. At his greeting, Dad stirs and shows his pleasure at the visit, then sleeps again. The doctor kisses my father and says goodbye. When he calls me and speaks with love of the man who was his friend, mentor and almost-father, his soft voice falters and breaks. He resumes: 'Howard, I am so thankful ...' He falls silent for a time, then he clears his throat and tries again. 'I'm glad I managed to see him ... and say goodbye.'

Dad is asleep, oblivious to suffering. Neither pain, nor odour, nor fear nor breathlessness troubles his rest.

All of my life, I have heard Dad speak enviously of those who die in their sleep. He sleeps now and as I sit alone by his bed this quiet night, I recall the death of his mother, and the deaths of his two younger brothers. All three died of kidney failure, a condition which brings about deepening drowsiness, then coma, then death. All died in their sleep.

It is very late. I decide to say my evening prayers at Dad's bedside. Since the day of his fall, I have been inserting into the liturgy a personal request for Dad's healing. I understand that at this stage, 'healing' can mean only one thing, and I submit to it. The prayers follow a formula in which I refer to my father by his Hebrew name and that of his mother: *May it be Your will to send perfect healing, a healing of the flesh and of the spirit, to Melekh ben Malka ...*

Dad's Hebrew name *Melekh* is something of a curiosity. It means 'king'; his mother's name, *Malka* means 'queen'. Thus Dad is 'King, son of Queen.'

In the quiet of this night, some lines from *Richard II* come to me that foretell the death of a king:

> Of comfort no man speak ...
> For God's sake let us sit upon the ground
> And tell sad stories of the death of kings ...

Although the text of my prayer carries a petition for healing of Dad's flesh, the deep wish that I breathe by his bedside is that my father will not again awaken to pain and to confusion. And when in due course my prayer will have been answered, I too will sit upon the ground and tell sad stories of the death of the 'king'.

I complete the evening service and, looking up, discover that Dad and I are not alone. There is another in the room with us – a short man with bushy whiskers. He sits without movement or speech, looking at my Dad. I recognise him from Dad's congregation. He is one of those whose first name Dad never knew. He wasn't one of Dad's intimates, just a man who must have valued him.

Dad was a shy man. When introduced to people, he would smile, take the offered hand and shake it, while averting his eyes sufficiently to avoid the eyes of the other. Dad could never imagine how he was respected by people he scarcely knew. He'd pour cold water on any suggestion that he had admirers. He'd have been quite at a loss to understand this man's visit.

The visitor rises to leave. He speaks briefly to me, bending over me. As he speaks, a large wet droplet falls onto my knee, then he is gone.

It is midnight. I say goodnight to Dad, kiss him, and go home to bed.

The phone rings at five in the morning. I catch it on the first ring. It's Jodie at the hospital. 'Howard. I am sorry to disturb you. I thought I should notify you; your father's breathing is slower, and his heart rate is slower too. I think you and the family should come to the hospital …'

I phone my brothers and tell them what I have heard. As I dress, I ask myself whether I should drop everything and rush to the hospital now, or follow my normal morning routine and risk losing this chance to see my father alive.

Somehow the decision does not feel critical. I am not afraid of missing a last opportunity to be close to Dad. My life has been that opportunity. I decide to brush my teeth and have my early morning thunderbolt espresso. I drink it, then drive to the hospital where I find my older brother and Jodie standing in the corridor. Jodie has been crying. She tells me that Dad stopped breathing a few minutes after she called.

'It was very fast,' she says. 'I am sorry …'

We enter Dad's room. I see his silent body, his still face. I watch and listen for a breath but there is none. He looks as if he is asleep.

Our younger brother Barry arrives and we stand and look in silence. It is not the unbearable experience we feared. It is simply a scene of peace. My older brother's voice says: 'I should go and get Mum.'

Some time later he returns, pushing Mum in her wheelchair. Her sons surround her, hold her and push her to Dad's side. She takes his hand, which is still warm. Her face is rent by grief. The mouth that kissed Dad is torn wide open in a soundless cry at the ending of all their years together. Her voice struggles to the surface as she weeps: 'He was a lovely man.'

As she sits and holds his hand, the minutes pass in silence, then she turns to us. Her face is whole again. Our mother looks at us and she sees only how life has blessed her. Her voice is happy as she says, 'Aren't I lucky to have my children?'

Now my tears come.

Hours pass. Dad's sons guard his body while we wait for Dr Campbell to arrive and to write his certificate of death. During this time my younger daughter Naomi phones and I go outside to meet her. It is a lovely September morning, clear and still – the sort of morning that gives spring its good name. My daughter embraces me and I too know how life has blessed me.

It is time for the morning prayer. I adorn myself with the full regalia – the *tallith* and the *tefillin* – and I sit on a bench in the park and say the prayers my father taught me. I return to the ward in a serene state.

During this interlude of prayer and loving reunion, someone has elected to stay by Dad's bedside, a final kindness, unthankable. From the last breath to the final sod at the funeral, the body is guarded, an act of honour for a human person.

The guard is Emma, my daughter-in-law.

Afterwards she says, 'I saw Dad two days ago, and he was in a stupor. He was groaning and gasping, his back was arched and he had flung himself uncomfortably close to the edge of the bed. It was a torment. Now he looks better; he is quiet and peaceful. I said goodbye and it felt like a moment of healing.'

My son Raphael waits for me in the corridor. He is not a man of speeches. His face says everything; his hazel eyes gaze steadily at me between red lids. He wants to see how I am doing. Stronger than his own grief is his concern for his father.

Dr Campbell bounds along the corridor towards us, a healthy young biped in spring. His ponytail swings as he approaches. His greeting is exuberant: 'How is your father doing today?'

When I tell him, his kind face fills with regret. 'I am so sorry … forgive me … I wasn't told.' He takes a deep breath.

David is not easily comforted. He is anxious to be helpful to us and is about to write the death certificate when his boss, the senior consultant in charge of Dad's care, calls him to a ward round. That consultant turns out to be a classmate from my medical school days. Encountering me in the corridor, he proffers formal regrets at Dad's passing: 'But he had a good run, didn't he?' – empty words to keep him safe from feeling, then changes the subject and speaks with animation about running, a mutual interest.

He goes off to save some lives and my son says, 'He's a bit of a tool, isn't he Dad?' For my part, I am grateful again that David Campbell was Dad's treating doctor.

Our father is dead. I understand the words, I am familiar with the concept, but I do not begin to comprehend it. The Hebrew word for the recently deceased is *niftar*. It means 'released'. I can comprehend that much.

The Jewish Burial Society – the Brotherhood of Loving Kindness and Truth as it is called – comes to take Dad away and to ensure that his body is treated with honour. It is time for us to part. '… the deep / Moans round with many voices.'

The Brotherhood is ready and this is my moment of farewell. I kiss Dad's forehead – the same forehead of so many Sabbath morning greetings in the synagogue. And I say, 'Goodbye, Dad. You have been a very good father to me.'

I pick up my bag and leave. A new idea comes to me: you haven't got a father anymore; you have to stand on your own now. And as I frame this thought, I find I am squaring my shoulders.

Raoul, it's me, Myer.

How did you get here, Myer?

I'm niftar, *Raoul; I'm free at last.*

The writer acknowledges the assistance of Messrs Shakespeare and Tennyson, and of Ms Dickinson.

A beginning

After they take my father's body away I drive from the hospital to a café in St Kilda. Here I meet a close friend whose mother died recently. In the crisis of her stroke he rushed to her bedside in England; she held on and he returned to Australia, only to turn around shortly afterwards to attend her funeral. His travels were frenetic. On his way home he paused at the seaside and found quiet. Here he wrote of his experiences, closing with the words: 'Once again I had occasion to say thank you to Mister Death.'

I am glad to talk to someone who has fresh acquaintance with Mister Death. He listens attentively as I describe Dad's passing. As

I repeat my parting words to Dad, his eyes fill with tears. When I describe Mum's grief he cries softly. My friend is doing my weeping for me.

I drive with my wife to the offices of the Chevra Kadisha. I have run past this place a thousand times, but I have never been inside. A Cohen is commanded to keep distant from the dead, so I've always crossed to the other side of the road, thankful for priestly purity. But when death comes as close as this, purity is put aside.

Annette has been here before. She takes my hand and we enter the office of the Director, who sits us down and speaks to us kindly. I know this guy. We bump into each other in the early mornings at the kosher bakery. There, his many friends make morbid jokes about his calling. And he replies, eyes sparkling, 'Never mind, you blokes – I'll get the lot of you when your time comes.'

Now he asks lots of questions. He wants to know Dad's date of birth, Dad's parents' names, his children's names and their dates of birth. He needs all these data for the Registrar of Births, Deaths and Marriages, but he asks many other questions in addition: Where are your father's parents buried? When did they die? Where were they married? In what year? And what about your mother's parents?

When I am unable to answer some of his questions, the Director consults his database of Jewish demographics. It is strangely moving to learn precise details about my mother's parents – whom I never met – from a man who never knew them. They are lost, but not without trace. They lived, they made my mother and my aunt and then they died young. And the Director of the Holy Society of Loving Kindness and Truth holds in trust the bones of their memory.

My sister Margot is not here yet. She makes her lonely odyssey across the skies from Budapest. She set out hoping to arrive in time to say goodbye to her father; she learned en route that Dad had died. She won't arrive until tomorrow morning.

It had been raining heavily in the weeks before 13 May 1949, and the Murrumbidgee flooded. The road from Narrandera to Leeton was cut and Mum's doctor couldn't come for Margot's birth. Mum came into labour on a Friday, and just before sunset Dad brought his daughter into the world. The Sabbath started and the man and the woman rested and saw the fruit of their labours and it was very good.

My brothers and I have been talking about the funeral: should one of us speak? When Margot calls from Los Angeles I ask her, 'Would you like to speak at the funeral tomorrow?'

The question takes her by surprise. She'll think about it.

Praying is a habit. Observant Jews like my father do it three times a day, emulating our patriarchs. The word we use for praying is *davening*. It means 'of, or like, the Fathers'. In my case it means of, or like, *my* father. I live the life of a Jew because of my father's teaching. I pray as my father prayed. And Dad prayed like his father.

Wrapped in his prayer shawl, my father stands in our lounge room and reads the silent devotion. As he *davens* Dad curls his fingers around the back of my neck, clasping me lightly. I stand close to him and wrap myself in his *tallith*, playing with the fringes, feeling the silken fabric on my front and the warmth of Dad's body against me.

Dad teaches me the Hebrew *alef-bet* – the alphabet – from his prayer book. The book is old, its pages stained, its leather cover worn by decades of daily use. 'Aunty Sophie and Uncle Sam gave me this as a bar mitzvah present,' he says.

He teaches me to pray. When I do so, he says I am a good boy; when I fail, I am not a good boy. And I fail pretty frequently. Those Hebrew consonants follow each other across the line in an orderly way, but the vowels lurk, now beneath, now above, now between the letters. It is very confusing. There are literally dozens of pages of prayers to be said, and it is a sore travail.

A child of four sometimes takes shortcuts in the prayer book, but this is cheating both God and Dad. Then Dad removes his caressing clasp from the back of my neck, and a painful lump rises in my throat. Dad seems to know whenever I cheat. Perhaps God tells him. Eventually, I decide that honesty pays: its dividend is father love. From then on I *daven* scrupulously.

Dad buys me a prayer book of my own and my own *tallith*. The book has a clean blue cover and the silk *tallith* is blue and white. Holding the book, wearing the *tallith*, I feel close to Dad. It is the same every time I use them. The time comes when I feel incomplete until I have said my prayers.

Now that my father is dead but not yet buried, I am told I am not to pray. I am an *onen*, one whose dead is before him, one supposed to be too distressed even to pray. But I want to pray. It is my habit – a garment, a practice, my abode. At prayer times that afternoon, that evening, next morning, I hanker to *daven* as usual. I want to feel connected with my father, not naked and homeless.

Annette says, 'I'm going to the airport.'

I don't want her to go. 'You don't have to go, you know. Margot said she'll take a cab. You don't know how long she'll be in customs ...'

'She's travelled for two days. She'll arrive and she'll know that this time she won't see her father alive. I'm going. And I'm going to take your mother too. They'll need to see each other. And I'll take her to the Chevra Kadisha to see your Dad's body if she wants.'

Our son has decided he will go to the airport too. He will help with the bags, he'll help with Mum's wheelchair, with anything. He realises that his status as a Cohen will keep him at the margins later, at the funeral. He wants to help.

Later when Annette's car pulls up, Margot steps out looking beautiful. She's wearing a black leather pants suit that sets off her ginger hair. She looks fresh and she feels good as she crushes me against her. She has seen Dad. 'I'm glad I went,' she says.

Mum has her daughter. I feel stronger, more complete. And Margot will feel more complete tomorrow when her son arrives from the States.

At the cemetery the first face I see belongs to my unblood brother, Johhny Wanklyn. Now a mountain of a man, he was just a wide grin beneath some freckles when I first met him in Leeton in 1950. Although I left Leeton for Melbourne in 1955, we have been close friends ever since.

He has driven here today from Albury. He is wearing a felt hat that is sublimely unfashionable. I climb out of the car and disappear into his embrace. The hat is his gesture to Jewish ritual. Happily, he is unaware that our practice is not to touch the mourners, whether in greeting or in consolation. This is the first time in our fifty-three years that I see that grin extinguished. His face is a battleground as he says, 'Doff – I'm not very good at these occasions.' He is trying not to cry. For myself, I am longing for tears.

Afterwards, when it is all over, I look about for my oldest friend. But he is not to be found. He is speeding home to Albury.

In June 1955 I am charged for the first time with my Jewish destiny. My older brother and I are about to leave Leeton for exile in Melbourne, where we will 'go to Mount Scopus and receive a Jewish education'. (I thought we were already receiving that education from my father. I think so still.)

We are standing on the doorstep of my oldest friend's house. We have come to say goodbye. His mother Dulcie takes me in her arms and holds me for a goodish while in her bosom. She does the same with my older brother. Then she speaks: 'You two boys have the duty to become the finest young Jewish gentlemen who ever were ... You owe it to your father and your mother ... *because of what they are giving up for your Jewish future.*'

Even though this comes from a lady who is not Jewish, it sounds like a commandment. It stays with me and I try to honour it. As we age, my older brother and I return from time to time to visit this lady, herself now very elderly, as if to assure her we are fulfilling her commandment.

Dulcie was born on 5 December 1909. That makes her exactly one year older than Dad. On Cup Day 1991, I visit her in Albury while I am recovering from surgery. She speaks of death and dying: 'Darling, I've seen a lot of death. I saw it when I was nursing – just as you do in your work. I was there when death came for my husband. When it comes, it's usually very gentle. It comes like the brush of a butterfly's wing against your cheek … then you fall asleep.

'Your father has to work; I don't think he can let himself retire. He has to serve, to help. He can't stop that. He'll keep going until he feels the touch of the butterfly's wing … and then he'll fall asleep.'

When Dulcie's turn came a year or two later, death was not so gentle. Her son has not got over it, so he is 'not very good at these occasions'. I don't think I have got over Dulcie's death either. I wish I could go and visit her again.

Here is someone whom I telephoned this morning in Brisbane. He stands to one side, a shrunken Falstaff. His characteristic volcanic mirth is stilled. Playing across his face are the shadows of the loss of his mother. My father's death has brought him here, in respect, in fellow grief. *After the first death there is no other.* He pays the cost of loving kindness.

Later, when the funeral ends, I look for him to offer comfort, but he is not to be found. He is in flight.

Hundreds of people come to honour Dad. They crowd into the small funeral chapel, spilling out the doors at the back and the sides. They are here from his youth, from his old age, from his synagogue and from his medical practice. I see many here who were never Dad's intimates. They all come to honour Dad.

A man from the burial society shows us how to rend our garments.

We make a tear in the fabric on the left side of the chest. 'Losing love / Is like a window in your heart / Everybody sees you're blown apart ...'

Margot speaks. Before her is our father's coffin. Beyond that, our mother and her brothers. The heavy silent room trembles. Across the silence Margot's voice is a crystal bell. It is poised, the elocution improved by decades in the States. Somewhat to our surprise, Margot says she prepared her remarks as she flew here from Istanbul. Some time later she makes a correction: 'Did I say Istanbul? I meant Budapest!'

Margot reviews Dad's life. She recalls Dad's father who arrived in Australia as a stowaway, aged twelve, in 1898. Far from his home and through a long life, our grandfather remained true to his faith. So too did his son.

She speaks of Dad the doctor, the farmer, the olive industry pioneer, the sailor, the chef, the servant of his community. She speaks with pride of these achievements and the bell rings clear and pure across the room. Then she speaks of the father, the son, the brother – and the bell cracks. No one minds.

Later Margot realises that she said nothing about Dad the husband, the tireless carer of our mother. She is stricken with regret. Afterwards many will say with wonder that Margot's speech was worthy of the man. It was a long life, it was a long speech. For many, both were too short.

Dad's old rabbi friend then reads psalms in Hebrew and in English. His voice is solemn, his utterance measured. When he reads scripture in translation, you imagine that the English text was given at Sinai together with the Hebrew, so harmonious are they together. And so perfectly pitched are they to work the wheels of awe and wonder.

The poetry undoes me. Now my longing for tears is requited. My daughters' eyes meet mine. They see me weep and are filled with concern for my loss and my pain. I wish I could tell them not to worry.

This is good grief; this pain is clean and sharp. It is due, it is meet … 'the toughest reserve, the slickest wit among us / trembles with silence, and burns with unexpected / judgements of peace.'

Then the rabbi gives his eulogy. He is an old man. His accent and slightly formal speech still bear traces of Europe. Delivered ponderously from deep in his breast, his words are born of labour, arriving in slow succession, each one fresh and warm and new, each deserving attention, like a litter of live-borns.

He says, 'I respected Myer deeply. In that I am one of many. Over many years I valued his medical attention and his friendship alike. I came to understand that in Myer these two were in fact the same thing.' The deep voice slows to a stop, then resumes. 'And … if I may confess it here … I loved Myer.'

Heads bow. Deep in their separate knowledge of loss, people are grieving – some for my father, some for another love; some for loss of love, others for lack of love.

The pallbearers take their stations. My younger brother breathes an anxious question into my ear: 'Are we ready for this?'

Four men begin a slow walk escorting Dad's body from the prayer room to the graveside. One of the four is Dad's oldest nephew; a second is the young doctor from Leeds; third and fourth are mates from Dad's synagogue. Week after week, the mates would stop by Dad's house and walk him to *shule*. They would not let him go alone. Now they take him on his last walk.

Dad's coffin rests on a sort of billycart, so this walk is actually a ride. My Mum rides too. She is in her wheelchair and I hold her hand, talking quietly to her as Annette pushes her. I am glad to look after Mum; there is relief in these simple acts. We follow the pallbearers from the perimeter pathway of the Cohen into unfamiliar territory. Rising around us on every side are the headstones I never saw from the roadway. I am walking alongside Mum, trying to look dignified and trying to look where I am going. This occupies my talents fully. Bending over Mum, whispering comfort close into her ears, I am dwarfed by the masonry. Looking up, looking around in awe, it's a bit like my first visit to New York. Absurd thoughts, unreal feelings.

This headstone is familiar: at its top is the name of my late father-in-law. Beneath his name is the Hebrew text which I helped to compose twenty years ago. I recall that task. It was pleasurable, a relief – like holding someone's hand. I recall too Dad's words around that time: 'Howard, I'm investing in real estate. I've bought a couple of plots next to Annette's father for Mum and me. Good location, convenient for the family … and I like the neighbourhood. Mum and I will spend eternity near Annette's parents.'

This excursion into the absurd is unexpected and disconcerting. I can't control it. Perhaps the absurd is helpful.

At the graveside now, we crowd around an open pit. The footing is uneven and the multitude at our backs and at our sides presses in. It occurs to me that one could fall in. It happened at another funeral we know of.

I look around. I want to ensure that we are all here – my mother, my brothers, Margot – all are close. But I want Annette close too, and my daughters. When Annette's father died, I was not close. I was standing at a distance, a Cohen, barred from the graveside by the rules of priestly purity, standing with my father and my son, kept far from Annette when she needed me.

Now my son stands at that distance, while I am at the edge of my father's grave. I feel for him. I look at the coffin. It seems an abstraction. It lacks emotional force. Stronger is the closeness to my loved ones.

Not panic, not a sense of awful finality at this next separation from Dad, but wholeness and support are the feelings that fill me. If I know anything, it is that the moment is unique in my fifty-seven years. I cannot reckon when or how this moment will come again. My mind stalls at the edge of the awful calculations.

As I think these things and refuse to think beyond, I feel Annette's arms around my chest. She stands behind me, embracing me, answering with her body the only questions necessary. I turn and locate Rachel and Naomi again. They are about two metres away. Their eyes rest upon their father's face; if they were pumping the blood inside my chest, they could not feel closer.

The pallbearers lower the coffin into the grave. Their faces are intent. They have no escape from the concrete reality with which we have entrusted them. What is friendship, that it exacts this toll?

A halt. Before us is a mound of clay. Two large shovels await their moment. Someone gestures, someone passes a handle towards us. The firstborn son takes a shovel first, hefts dirt, slings it forward. The clods pass through air – forward, downward, landing upon hollow board. A sound replies, an ordinary sound, a sound of this world. The sound does not tear me apart as they said it might. Gently, we pass the handle to Mum and help her with the task of burying her husband. Then it is my turn, my sister's, my younger brother's. Each helps the other, all defer, each trembles for the frailty of our flesh. A terrible tenderness is born.

Now cousins, now second cousins, now in-laws, friends, old men, young men, take, bend and heave, joining in the yeomanry. Some take the shovel and work with a fever, not in token, but work hard until the sweat runs, until the task is done.

The grave is filled. Backs straighten and another silence falls. Then the rabbi motions to the sons to recite *Kaddish*. This is the mourner's prayer. Dad's sons will recite it in a synagogue, at three services every day for the next eleven months. *Yitgadal v'yitkadash sh'mai rabah* … May the name of the Great One be magnified and sanctified …

A synagogue-goer knows this opening phrase intimately, its rise and its fall. It is as if a congregation inhaled and exhaled. It is the familiar breathing of the praying body. And here are Dad's three sons, all of us liturgically competent, each holding a copy of the text, all of us stumbling as we clamber through the *Kaddish*. We have no rhythm. The Aramaic text tricks and trips us. We reach the final sentence: 'May He who makes peace in His high places, make peace upon us ...'

We get to the end and I have no regret for our stumbling. It is meet. There will be time in the months to come for facile skill. For now, I am content to make my way, alongside my brothers and my sister, through clod and rubble and a toilsome path from this place.

Why say *Kaddish*? It is, after all, an everyday prayer as much as it is the prayer of mourning. It is everyman's prayer. What has it to do with grief, with me, with Dad? It doesn't speak of death or loss or of comfort. It simply declares its theological verities, here, at the edge of life. It faces quite resolutely away from human sorrow. Why bother with it? What good is it to me?

But I feel its action by the end of the very first phrase. My brothers and I pause and anticipate what follows; the entire congregation responds 'Amen'. This response, a soft tide of exhalation, says: 'You are not alone in this ritual of mourning by not mourning.' When we pause at the end of each phrase, 'Amen' flows from each breast. Our grieving is reciprocal.

As we wheel Mum away from the grave, I remark that I have never previously been at the graveside. Her reply surprises me: 'Neither have I, darling.'

'Really, Mum? What about when your parents were buried?'

'I didn't go. Doreen and I stayed home. Children weren't supposed to go to burials. And later, when I went to funerals as an adult, I stayed away from the grave ... I didn't want to be there.' Mum holds my hand.

Afterwards, we return to Mum's place – it used to be Mum and Dad's place, but now it's just Mum's – and we are served the mourners' first meal. It starts with an egg. An egg is the precursor of life. It implies life. It is finite while its curved surface is endless, just as life is at the same time finite and endless. It is supposed to make you think.

Among other things it makes me think of a real meal. And a real meal is not long in coming. Our wives, our cousins, our children have reverted to hyper-catering, the invariable response of Jewish women to deep emotion. In the coming days I respond by hyper-eating. Months later I am still filling a deep pit.

After the meal, I take an apple. Like all modern apples, this one has grown with a little adhesive label that identifies the brand. Crunching into the flesh, I think of Dad eating his last apple … We are in the hospital. Dad has rallied. He asks for an apple and I hand him one. 'Peel it please,' he says.

'Don't you eat the peel, Dad?'

'No … never have … all my life.'

I take the flimsy plastic knife that comes with the kosher meal and laboriously butcher the apple out of its skin. Before Dad can start to eat, the doctor arrives and the apple is put aside. He does his doctoring and departs.

Dad then begins eating voraciously. I notice that it is the skin of the apple that Dad is eating and he is enjoying it. I notice also that he is at this moment biting into the label. When I point it out to Dad he says mildly, 'It doesn't taste too bad.' Now all apple labels remind me of Dad, of his gusto and his quirky humour.

After dinner, people come for the evening service. They crowd into Mum's house and stand before us as we mourners sit on low seats in our torn clothes. We mourners sit and pray, the comforters stand and pray.

I am chosen to lead the prayers. It feels good to pray again. At the end of the short service, my brothers and I recite *Kaddish*. I move away from the front to be closer to my brothers. Our three voices are one. I say the words and I hear the words from my older brother's throat and from the throat of my younger brother. We read softly but the quiet multitude hears us and responds, then we pick up the prayer until it is their turn again. Three subdued male voices, and behind our voices and above, a softer, sweeter voice shadowing ours, whispering, keeping pace. Is it Margot, claiming a prerogative to recite this prayer of the men, along with her brothers?

We four are playing hockey at our childhood home, Margot is the only girl in our marathon games as we hack and chop at the ball, slashing with equal indifference at Dad's azaleas and each other's legs.

Margot emerges from these games and plays hockey at school – a spirited and dauntless competitor. Her female schoolmates quail before her. The State selectors invite her to try out for Victoria. But she will not – the trials are on the Sabbath.

If Margot wants to *daven* with the men, so be it. She has earned it. But I do not look over my shoulder to investigate. I do not enquire until months later when Margot and I are talking on the phone: 'Do you say *Kaddish,* Mig?'

'No, I never felt the need.'

(Whose then was that voice?)

Three times a day, we conduct prayer services in the *shiva* house, which is Mum's home. We recite *Kaddish* at every service and, standing between my brothers, saying this prayer with them, I feel peace. Dad would love to see this: his three boys, contentious and individualistic by nature, by no means uniformly observant, all united in this prayer. It is a familiar experience.

We are children. All four of us are standing in the synagogue. The cantor is singing the *Kaddish* in his rich tenor. He comes to the end of a phrase and we four belt out the responses at the top of our voices. We know how to read the words and we quickly learn the tunes. We sing along with Dad and Uncle Abe. In a congregation of spectators we are conspicuous players.

Our voices ring. Dad and Uncle Abe look at each other and smile, then they tell us stories about their own synagogue childhood. 'We three brothers' (they recall) 'used to sing louder than anyone else.

Everybody said, "That's the Goldenberg Boys!"' My father and uncle are proud of us. We are just like *they* were. I feel proud too.

In the days that follow, the seven days of *shiva*, visitors come throughout the day and into the evening to offer comfort. There is a protocol: we mourners – that is, Mum and her children – sit on low chairs, in slippered feet and the torn garments we wore to the funeral. We don't shave, nor drink wine, nor work, cook or attend to business. People come and sit, on normal chairs, close to us. They are not supposed to initiate conversation but to listen to anything we might wish to say, and to respond. But they do say things. For seven days, they say the things they want us to know.

'Your father was a great man …'

'You have no idea how much your old man influenced my life …'

'Your father saved me when I was a teenager; he made my old man lighten up and let me have some fun …'

'I will miss him …'

'Myer looked after me and the children after my husband died …'

'When I couldn't pay my kids' school fees, your old man stood guarantor to the school. When I still couldn't pay at the end of term, the school was going to kick the kids out, but your father paid …'

'He wouldn't let anybody help him as he pushed your mother's wheelchair into our clinic. He had to do it all – and he was ninety-two years old!'

'He circumcised all our boys; he wouldn't take any money …'

'Your father lived his faith, daily, without excuse or deviation …'

'I was awed by your father's great strength …'

'I was inspired by his vitality …'

'I respected him …'

The sweetest pleasure of my boyhood was always to hear an adult praise Dad or Mum. This week of *shiva* is seven days in paradise for a child of Myer Goldenberg. Every kind word loosens the tides of tears. And the tides wash clean and clear the memories of my fifty-seven years as Dad's son.

Visitors are not supposed to bring little children into a house of mourning, because a child is so delightful that the mourner might neglect the real agenda, which is loss. Happily for me, we live in times of great religious ignorance. My grandson Jesse, aged ten months, arrives and makes a beeline for his grandfather on his low stool. I play with him and he plays with me. He climbs up on me and removes my *yarmulke* then replaces it. He does this repeatedly, losing his footing often and tumbling into my arms, looking up, gurgling and beaming, before climbing again for another assault upon the headgear.

Ellie, aged four months, is a softer proposition. When she visits she needs to be held, or, more accurately, I need to hold her. She has cheeks like the ripest apricots which must be kissed. She has lips that are cherries that have to be tasted. This imperative sweetness quite undoes all mourning.

I hold these, our hatchlings, and I reflect upon my father, patriarch of this tribe. In his last year or so, he held all four of his new great-grandchildren in his arms. He knew their sweetness; he knew he was blessed. I feel the sadness of losing Dad. I will never again see my long-time friend. But life is not empty. I know it, not least because my father taught me.

I look at these babies. If one of them were to be lost, I would lose faith in life. I would not know how to live.

I am dreaming about Dad. A group of us is lounging around on the grass; it feels like a family picnic. We are relaxed and happy. Dad lies on his side a few metres in front of me, enjoying the sunshine. He is wearing his pale blue-green jumper.

Dad always had difficulty with blue and green; he could tell that they were different, but he could not nominate the respective colours reliably. So here he is in my dream, at his ease, in his ambiguous jumper, his sons and others around him.

I am taking my leave. I say, 'Dad, I'm going now. I'm going to do some writing.'

Dad rolls over on his side turning from me to my brothers. His voice is affectionate as he says warmly, 'He drives me crazy with his writing.'

I awaken from my dream. Although Dad has gone, the warmth of the scene stays with me. Dad always dismissed my memoirs as fictions, but privately he took delight in them. Out of my hearing he spoke proudly about my writing. And now in my dream, he's at it again – speaking words of rejection that have no sting.

Friday comes and, with it, the approach of *Shabbat,* which temporarily suspends mourning. By some instinct, the whole clan gathers at Mum's place for dinner on Friday night. We will celebrate this *Shabbat* like any other, with rejoicing, with song, with best clothes and food. No low stools, no slippers, no torn garments. From sunset Friday until three stars are seen on Saturday night, joy will take over from grieving. Then we will sit *shiva* again.

We all feel we should be near Mum to support her. But who will recite *kiddush* – the Sabbath prayer of dedication – that Dad always sang? *Kiddush* is always more than a song.

Something happens on Friday evenings: Dad is in a special mood. He wants everything to be done right – the prayers said and the candles lit on time and the Sabbath table set and all the weekday concerns put away. He sings a mystical song to welcome the Sabbath bride, then reads the evening prayers, and ends with songs to welcome the angels that attend us on the Sabbath. His voice is sweet and the tunes are melodious and sad. We learn to sing with Dad.

Darkness is coming down and I wait, overtired, laced tight to my family, expectant, irritable with hunger, sensitive – waiting for the relief of tears or of blessing.

Dad finishes his prayers. Now he stands us up and blesses us. He does it in order of our age – firstborn first, then me, then our little sister, then the baby. Dad puts his hands on our heads and says the words softly in Hebrew. During the blessing I feel the texture of the corduroy warm against my forehead. Dad is intense and very tender as he recites the blessing.

May the Lord bless you and keep you.

May the Lord light up His countenance towards you and be gracious to you.

May the Lord lift up His countenance to you and give you peace.

The last word is *shalom*. Then Dad kisses us.

Dad stands at the head of the table and Mum stands at the opposite end. When Dad sings the *kiddush* he holds the goblet in his right hand. He has the curious habit of holding his left arm behind his back. When I discover this, I place my hand into his palm and Dad holds it there until the end when he raises the goblet, says the blessing and drinks. Then we all drink – Mum first and the children in order of age. The wine is sweet and strong. I shiver as I swallow it. Long after becoming an adult with children of my own, I like to stand behind Dad, my hand enclosed in his, while he recites *kiddush*.

And now here we are again at the *Shabbat* table – the table that Dad himself built – and here is Dad's *kiddush* cup, but Dad is not here. We all stand. A quietness falls upon us while we take it in. I feel suddenly anxious. The firstborn brother is not keen on singing a *kiddush* solo, so the brothers all take a glass and we sing it together.

Kiddush is going along pretty well – there's Mum, held close by her grandchildren; here are my kids, their spouses, my grandbabies and Annette. The voices of the Goldenberg boys are rising and falling in unison – when I sense a trembling at my side. I glance at Annette; her lips are quivering. I follow her gaze across the table to my son whose eyes look funny. One after another, faces face faces, and the closing benediction is said hastily while voices begin to choke and break.

As I drink I realise that I haven't come here to look after Mum. I have come here to be looked after. Unsurprisingly, *Shabbat* is as joyous as ever – just more intense.

After *Shabbat* we resume *shiva*. Protocol restricts touching. Wives and husbands are denied intimate touch, and visitors do not touch the mourners. During our week of *shiva*, this practice is observed in the breach. Happily unaware, our visitors express themselves by bodily demonstration. My cousins clasp my hand and hug me; women sweep me into their warm embrace; cousins' daughters, nieces and nephews all kiss me. This suits my temperament perfectly. The kindly impulse of these rule-breakers satisfies some maverick strain within me. Others – who accept the disciplines of silence and distance, obliged to gaze wordlessly into my face and to accept the burden of my grief – these please me too with their level courage.

After one of the prayer services, Hugo and his father pay a visit. Hugo is a small boy with eyes like baby eggplants. He listens gravely as his father tells him that Howard's Daddy isn't alive anymore. His mouth is open as he takes it all in. '… and Howard's Daddy got so sick and so old he couldn't live anymore.'

'What happened then, Daddy?'

Daddy says, 'I'm not sure. What do you think happened, Howard?'

'I think my father fell asleep.'

A few weeks later, Hugo is sitting in the back of his father's car when he says, 'I hope you don't die. I hope Mummy doesn't die …' A pause, then: 'I think Howard will be all right. I think he'll get a new Daddy.'

It is the seventh day. I awaken to birdsong just as I did every morning last spring. I heard this selfsame song after the birth of my grandson. I lie in bed and listen to the sounds until it is time to get up and go to the final *shiva* service.

Dad's young rabbi friend comes to the house. At the end of the service the brothers recite *Kaddish,* then the visitors disperse and hurry off to work, to school, to life.

The young rabbi speaks to us mourners on our low chairs. He utters the formal command to joy: 'Arise from your mourning. May you be comforted among those who mourn for Zion and Jerusalem ... May you know no further sorrow.'

He leaves, Margot flies to the airport, we brothers go to work.

Mum stays.

I take the train, get off at my usual station and walk along the underpass. From the far end I hear a sound like a human voice raised in lament. It is a busker, playing *klezmer* music on the cello. The sound is unbearably lovely. I walk to the café. They bring me my usual latte, strong, hot, lots of froth. I sit and raise the cup to drink when a friendly voice calls out, 'Howard!'

I search the café for a face to fit the warm feminine sound that caresses my ears. There, against the opposite wall, is Jenny. Jenny and her husband hire out the yachts that Dad and I have sailed on the Gippsland Lakes for the last fifteen years. The last time I saw her, Dad was farewelling her and her husband after another sailing trip. That was seven months ago ...

Dad stands on the gravel verge of the roadway, facing Jenny and Fred, facing the sea that sparkles beyond them in the sunshine. Dad's back is to me. I retire to the car so I can record the scene in my notebook: 'Dad stands and speaks. Jenny and Fred lean to this precious old man, by far the oldest of the many who sail their fleet. He has had a wonderful time. He is saying thank you and goodbye – goodbye to sailing, goodbye to the sea.'

I put down my book. I cannot write any more ...

Jenny says, 'I have come up to town to see the accountant. How wonderful to see you. Tell me – how is your father?' I tell her. Her hand flies to her mouth. I look for words to comfort her.

Back at work again, kindly faces surround me. They search my face and find with relief that I am not broken. Each asks, 'How are you doing?' My eyes sting. It feels like the splash of sea water in my eyes as Dad drives the boat hard into an oncoming wave.

After seeing a few patients I pick up the phone, obedient to my morning reflex; I'll just ring Dad and find out how he and Mum are going. Then I remember. I put down the phone and start to write. I am thinking about Dad and about Raoul Wallenberg. I pause and smile as I think how Dad would dismiss my whimsical essays into the imagination.

I'm free, Raoul. And I've set the others free, all of them: the boys, Margot, Yvonne too ... They're free now. It's the last thing I can do for them.

The author thanks Dylan Thomas, Paul Simon and Les Murray for the consolations of their verse during shiva.

Glossary of Jewish terms

Ashkenazi

A term used broadly for Jewish people of European extraction. Its literal meaning is 'German', from the ancient Hebrew word *ashkenaz*, in Genesis, which might or might not refer to that portion of Europe.

Ashkenazi Jews tend to have a European appearance, due doubtless to the donation (often unwelcome and by force of rape) of genes from the host country in Europe. We Ashkenazis share genes that predispose us to various inherited diseases, such as Amaurotic familial idiocy (Tay-Sachs Disease). Ashkenazi Jews follow one or another of the European liturgies, in distinction to the rituals and liturgies of the Jews of North African extraction (called Sephardis).In the plural we are Ashkenazim.

Bar mitzvah

Literally, 'son of the commandment', but better understood as 'youth of commandment age'. It refers to that age (thirteen years) when a Jewish male assumes responsibility for his own religious conduct. The attainment of the age of bar mitzvah is marked by synagogue observances in which the boy carries out rituals which are reserved for adults. In this sense, he is now a man.

The boy then leaves the synagogue – often disappearing until his marriage – and reaps the fruits of his studies. In my day these were wristwatches and fountain pens; now they are computers, electronic games and i-Pods.

There is a party at which the adults eat lots of food and the boy's friends throw it at each other.

Bat mitzvah

Literally, 'daughter of the commandment', analogous to bar mitzvah in all respects, excepting for synagogue ritual. Among the Orthodox, a bat mitzvah observance in synagogue used to be a token event in my childhood, but nowadays a girl might study seriously and deliver an earnest lecture or homily, sometimes composed by herself. A bat mitzvah girl usually scores a new outfit to mark her majority.

Brith (bris, brith millah)

Literally, 'a covenant'. It is not a surgical term but it is a surgical event: a ritual circumcision, performed upon a male Jewish child on the eighth day of life. There is no surgery for females in Judaism. The full name of the event is *Britho shel Avraham avinu*, the covenant of Abraham our father.

A *brith* is a great celebration for all who attend (except the *brithee* and his mum). Men attending a *brith* relieve their anxiety by cracking jokes. Some men faint. After the surgery, whisky and herrings are consumed. The baby is given a finger dipped in wine to suck. Invariably this stops the baby crying. The baby then accepts a breast feed which sometimes stops the mother crying.

Chevra Kadisha

A shortened form of *Chevra Kadisha shel Hessed Ve'emeth*, the Sacred Society of Loving Kindness and Truth. (In truth, Hebrew lacks capital letters, but they would be very proper nouns.)

The Chevra (to pronounce the 'ch', forget goat's cheese; think of Bach) Kadisha is the Burial Society, a bunch of people who perform the very last rites, *tahara* (purification by bathing) and shrouding of the body. These people are unpaid volunteers. Their actions are deemed *hessed*, or loving kindness, because the deceased can neither know nor thank them for their actions. In this sense, the members of the burial society are altruists whose deeds – which might daunt others – are sacred.

Chuppah

The nuptial canopy, symbolic of the marital home or even the marital bed, beneath which Jewish couples wed. (Don't even begin to try to pronounce it by the rules of English pronunciation: its first sound is the 'ch' as in Bach, and it rhymes (incongruously) with 'pooper'.

Daven

To pray (from the Aramaic that refers to the *Avoth*, the three patriarchs, Abraham, Isaac and Jacob who, in scripture, inaugurated one or other of the three daily prayer services). When one *davens*, one is worshipping in the tradition of the Fathers. In my own case – and I believe in my father's – *davening* linked me in fidelity to the father of flesh and blood who raised me and taught me to *daven*, as much as it did to the biblical patriarchs.

Eicha

Literally, 'How? …' *Eicha* is the name and the first word of the Scroll of Lamentations, putatively authored by the prophet Jeremiah, which recalls and bewails the sack of Jerusalem and the destruction of the Temple in Jerusalem.

Ellul

The last month of the Jewish calendar year, usually corresponding to September. Ellul precedes the period of the High Holydays – *Rosh Hashanah* (New Year) and *Yom Kippur* (the Day of Atonement). In a bad year, one or other of these holy days falls on Grand Final day, the last Saturday in September. When this happens, Collingwood usually loses.

Like the names of the other months, the name Ellul is Persian.

Haggadah

The most popular of Jewish religious books, it tells the story (*Haggadah* means 'a telling') of enslavement in Egypt, and liberation and exodus under the leadership of Moses. The *Haggadah* has been published in numberless editions, usually decorative, often intentionally pitched at the young for the purpose of stimulating their interest.

Many Jewish adults treasure the *Haggadah* of their childhood, wine-stained, tattered, chockers with family and folk memory.

Hebrew

The name given to the language of the Jewish Bible, also the name given to the Jewish people before they returned to the Promised Land after the exodus from Egypt. Abraham was the first Hebrew or *Ivri*, a word derived from the verb *la'avor*, to cross or to pass. Abraham crossed from the riverland of Iraq and passed to the Land of Canaan. He and his descendants became Hebrews.

Hebrew, being the language of scripture, is regarded as sacred, so much so that, following its rebirth as a lingua franca, many devout Jews refused to use it for any secular purpose.

Goy

In the original Hebrew, a nation. When used in Yiddish, it betokens a member of one of the non-Jewish nations of the earth, i.e. a gentile. The plural is *goyim*, as in 'what will the *goyim* say?'

Kaddish

The name given to a prayer in Aramaic declaring the greatness of God. The mourner's prayer is one of the various forms of *Kaddish*. It does not mention grief, death, sorrow or consolation, simply addressing the sanctity and the eternity of the Creator. Jews of just about every stamp, from devout to secular to atheistic, are likely to recite or to respond to the *Kaddish* at the time of bereavement, if only to express solidarity with the bereaved and with the generations of Jews who recited this prayer at such a time.

The name *Kaddish* refers to holiness.

Kiddush

Another prayer, this in Hebrew, whose name is derived from the word for holy. The Hebrew concept of the holy is derived from the verbal form, *le'kadesh* which denotes to dedicate, to set aside, to mark as sacred.

Kiddush is recited before the festive meals of the Sabbath and the festivals, and includes the blessing over wine.

Kosher

Literally, 'fitting, suitable, conforming to a norm'. Kosher food conforms to the dietary laws which are detailled and mandatory. There is no biblical basis for the modern notion that the purpose of the laws of kosher food is for good health. On the contrary, one can achieve impressive obesity and, with persistence, diabetes, on a kosher diet. Kosher foods, wines, marriage partners and ethical conduct broadly seem pointed to tribal solidarity and to a striving for the elevation of human life.

Megillah (pl. Megilloth)

Literally, scroll. There are five *megilloth* that are read in the synagogue, each at its own season in the Jewish calendar.

Eicha is read on the Fast of *Tisha B'Av*; Esther at *Purim*, and so on. Each *megillah* has a distinctive and traditional cantillation.

Mezuzah

Literally, a doorpost, a lintel. In ordinary usage a *mezuzah* is the parchment fragment, usually enclosed in an ornamental case, that is affixed to the doorpost or gatepost of a Jewish home or business. It is a talisman, guarding our comings and goings. A *mezuzah* on the door attracts collectors for charity in their droves. The parchment scroll is inscribed with the words of the *Shema*, the creed that declares the Jew's utter and absolute monotheism.

Mohel

A ritual circumcisor. Traditionally, a *mohel* was not a doctor but a learned and pious man, trained in the craft. In far-flung communities like Melbourne, the *mohel* often doubled as a ritual slaughterer (*shochet*). My own *mohel* was also a *shochet*.

A *mohel* earned his living by performing *brith millah*. My father carried out thousands of ritual circumcisions and never charged for them. Instead, he requested that the families make a donation to an educational institution. Dad was honoured repeatedly for his charity and his skill.

(If you elect to have yourself circumcised at the Mizrachi Synagogue in Melbourne, you will be placed upon a 'throne of Elijah the prophet', a specially-made chair designed for this ceremony, which bears a plaque inscribed by his grandchildren in honour of Myer Goldenberg.)

Mordechai

The hero of the *Purim* story, as described in the *megillah* of Esther.

Sephardi (Sefardi)

A Jewish person of North African lineage; the liturgy of this group. Sephardim are of Middle Eastern appearance. Following the establishment of the State of Israel, many Sephardim became refugees and fled to Israel. Few remain in the Muslim countries where they had lived for centuries.

Shabbat (Shabbos)

The Sabbath (the English word is a transliteration of the Hebrew). The Sabbath day commemorates the completion of the creation of the universe. Work (i.e. creative labours as defined in minute detail in rabbinic legislation) is forbidden. It is a day of physical and spiritual recreation in which one refrains from work, eats better food, wears better clothing, takes more time for prayer and religious learning, spends time enjoyably with family and friends, and (in the case of a male) takes time and trouble to give sexual pleasure to his wife. It is a day of great joy, and families treasure it.

Shabbat is referred to as 'a sort of paradise'. The aphorism is: more than the Jew has kept the *Shabbat*, the *Shabbat* has kept the Jew.

Shalom

Literally, peace. Jews greet and farewell each other with this word (precisley analogous to the Islamic practice in a related word or phrase), and reiterate it in prayer as an ideal, characterised by a messianic age, and as a supreme blessing.

Shiva

Literally, seven. The term refers to the initial seven-day period of mourning that follows a burial. First degree relatives sit on low stools for these seven days – hence, sitting *shiva* – neither going out to work, nor shaving, nor cooking nor engaging in conjugal sexual relations. It doesn't sound like much fun, but Jews of all degrees of religious observance derive enormous comfort from the structured space for grieving that the *shiva* period provides.

Shule (Shul, Schule)

Synagogue, Jewish house of worship and of religious learning; derived from the German for 'school'.

Succah, Succoth

A *succah* is a booth, a sort of dodgy cubby house with a roof of foliage which must be neither rain- nor sun-proof. For seven days during the festival of rejoicing that is Tabernacles (*Succoth*), Jewish people reside in the *succah* and rejoice in divine Providence. It is a fabulous festival.

Tallith

A prayer shawl, a rectangular garment with ritual fringes attached to its four corners. Traditionally, this poncho-like garment was made of wool and dyed with a specific mystical blue, now lost. In my growing up, a *tallith* was made of silk and was more like a scarf than a poncho. I must be one of legion Jewish children with fond memories like mine, of enfolding myself in Dad's *tallith* while he *davened*.

In my childhood the silk scarf style was worn in Jewish congregations of the Anglo-German tradition. Jews of Eastern European background looked down on this as Anglo-Danglow affectation and as ritually effete. Nowadays Jews across the orthodox spectrum tend to favour the woollen article of older tradition.

Tisha B'Av

The fast of the ninth day of the month of Av, a miserable day when Jews remember the loss of the Temple in Jerusalem. We sit on low stools, read *Megilloth Eicha* (Lamentations) and sad songs (including beautiful elegies in Hebrew verse written during the Golden Age of Jewry in Moorish Spain).

For twenty-five hours we neither eat nor drink. Showering, the use of deodorant, the wearing of leather footwear, kissing and sexual intercourse are all proscribed. In Israel, the fast occurs in the heat of summer; in Australia in the cold and gloomy depths of winter. No matter where you observe it, there is not much good about the day except for the poetry.

Torah

The Five Books of Moses, or Pentateuch. Torah can refer to Biblical literature generally, and is also used to refer to the Oral Law (*Torah sheh b'al Peh*) which incorporates the Talmud. In Jewish teaching, Torah represents the written record of the mind of God. It is immutable, authoritative and, of course, sacred.

A Torah scroll is a holy and precious item. It represents about a year's work of a trained scribe (*sofer*), so it doesn't come cheap. One who drops a Torah scroll fasts for forty days as a penance; likewise anyone unlucky enough to be present when it falls.

Tzitzith (Zitzith)

Ritual fringes. The strings you see dangling from the four-cornered undershirt of the observant Jewish male; also the fringes attached to the prayer shawl (*tallith*) worn at morning prayers. They are a visible reminder to the wearer to observe the laws of the Torah.

Yarmulke

A skullcap. Jews of the author's generation use this (Yiddish/Polish/Turkic) word where following generations are more likely to employ the modern Hebrew *kippah*. The latter is more appropriate, but old *yarmulkes* tend to stick. The head covering is held to symbolise a reverent awareness of a higher being.

Males wear *yarmulkes* for prayer, while women who cover their heads do so for modesty. Orthodox males tend to keep their heads covered during waking hours, simply because reverence seems always desirable and because the wearer is always about to break into prayer.

A Jewish male will don his *yarmulke* on awakening and keep it on until after the bedtime prayer. The *yarmulke* is removed for showering and removes itself during bedtime exertions.

The author's *yarmulke* also falls off during pap tests.

www.ingramcontent.com/pod-product-compliance
Lightning Source LLC
Chambersburg PA
CBHW060020100426
42740CB00010B/1542